Y0-BVO-151

Making
Wage Incentives Work

Making Wage Incentives Work

H. K. von Kaas

in collaboration with A. J. Lindemann

American Management Association, Inc.

International standard book number: 0-8144-5251-5
Library of Congress catalog card number: 75-138572

First printing

Preface

Wage incentive plans have made a major contribution toward increased productivity, lowered costs, and the enhancement of employee income, yet their acceptance has not been universal. In fact, although work measurement technology has improved remarkably since 1950, the number of installations of wage incentives has been relatively static since the 1960s. More than that, the histories of many incentive installations reveal that dissatisfaction often develops several years after the time of installation. On examination, the dissatisfaction is usually found to be not necessarily caused by the plan itself; very frequently it arises from the administration and maintenance of the plan rather than from the design of the plan or the work measurement function.

Top management people are seldom aware of the basic principles and techniques of good wage incentive administration. They generally are familiar with the arithmetic of the particular plan in use at their plant and with the operating results in terms of incentive gains and coverage, but they are becoming increasingly irritated by the various manifestations of a malfunctioning wage incentive plan—grievances, controlled production rates, controlled earnings, failure to perform at true incentive pace, and clerical costs of administering the plan.

Management people are frequently unfamiliar with the effect of policy decisions on such matters as incentive adjustments, personnel administration, settlement of rate grievances, and union contract clauses relating to the operation of the wage incentive plan and associated management activities. Very few executives appreciate the need for thorough maintenance and auditing of their incentive plans.

There are numerous excellent textbooks on work measurement and on wage incentive plans. However, in most cases they are technically oriented and concerned largely with the work measurement function and the initial design of wage incentive plans. In that respect, they are largely addressed to the practicing industrial engineer. This book, therefore, is directed toward a better understanding of the administrative aspects of wage incentive plans, the adaptability of specific plans to various types of work done, and a discussion of maintenance and auditing procedures necessary to prevent deterioration of the plan. For that reason, discussions of techniques and measurement procedures have been kept at a minimum and the emphasis is on the successful operation of incentive plans.

With this in mind, the first chapter discusses the general background and development of wage incentives in our industries and develops basic policies that must be formulated and administered to keep the plan operating properly. Subsequent chapters deal with the suitability of specific types of wage incentives to various broad kinds of work done in industry. Following this, the writer outlines techniques and procedures for evaluating performance of existing plans in terms of earning patterns and statistical backgrounds as well as the capabilities of the industrial engineering function and the shop administration.

Further discussions deal with general administrative problems, the effect of union contract clauses relating to incentives, and suggestions for improvements in this relationship. Procedures for modernizing the incentive plan and upgrading the industrial engineering department will also be discussed. The writer feels that modern statistical techniques and computer aids to standards development, together with new computer-aided techniques for indirect work measurement, make a significant contribution to management.

In developing the principal topic of this book, treatment of the activities and purposes of the industrial engineering department has been restricted to discussion of proper work measurement practices and effective wage administration. Measurement in general, and more specifically work measurement, has so many other uses that it has become a significant management tool. Measurement of some kind is vital to the operation of any enterprise whose success is based on proper relation of inputs (labor, material, overhead) and outputs (product shipped or services produced). Any discussion of industrial engineering functions and activities must be based on a knowledge of the varied uses of work measurement, and that is supplied by Appendix D, "Uses of Work Measurement."

The book is written from a background of over forty years of designing, developing, administering, and auditing a variety of wage incentive plans in many different industries. The background includes assignments as chief industrial engineer and as chief manufacturing engineer in several multiple-plant organizations followed by ten years as management consultant in those same areas and several years of part-time teaching and lecturing on these and related topics at the graduate level in the University of Wisconsin–Milwaukee.

The author gratefully acknowledges the valuable assistance of his collaborator, Professor A. J. Lindemann, the contributions of W. L. Kern, Parker Dumbauld, William Gleason, Jerry Kovach, and James Gear of Management Science, Inc., and the help of James Thorp, Egon Peck, Glenn Wolfe, and Dr. Russell Fenske.

A special acknowledgment is due Merlyn L. Koth for her valuable assistance in transcribing, organizing, and editing the numerous tape recordings, rough drafts, and other materials used in developing the book.

H. K. von Kaas

Contents

1

Wage Incentives: Theory and Practice

The problem of properly rewarding a man for his services is as old as recorded history. It continues to be one of the most important and certainly one of the most difficult of all our industrial problems. The interest in making more money and in the things that money can buy is a predominant influence—particularly in America. Not every individual has the desire to make more money, and there are variations in the intensity of that desire, but the fact remains that money can buy both luxuries and the many devices that make life easier and more enjoyable.

Some may argue that the urge to accumulate more money declines after a man's physiological and safety needs have been satisfied. That may be true to some extent, but it is also true that money is an important means of satisfying a man's social needs, such as the esteem of his peers, and providing for the enjoyment of the leisure time that has been given him by longer vacations and a shortened work-week. The result has been a phenomenal increase in purchases of sporting goods, fishing equipment, camping trailers, small pleasure boats, color television, and stereo and in vacation travel by all segments of the population.

Effect of Wage Incentives

The desire for greater income has been reflected in demands for greater and greater wage increases by both industrial and nonindustrial employees. There is no foreseeable possibility of a decrease in those wage demands, and they are also frequently directed toward a loosening of wage incentives. The result is increased pressure on profit margins, particularly when it is difficult to simply increase prices to cover increased labor costs, and so an analysis of measures to increase productivity assumes vital importance.

It is a well-accepted fact that the introduction of wage incentives has resulted in remarkable increases in productivity and corresponding reductions in cost. When wage incentive plans are successfully applied and administered, they also result in considerably enhanced employee earnings and industrial profitability. The procedures of work measurement have been continuously improved by the use of such techniques as predetermined time systems, standard data development, and, more recently, standard time development by the use of computers. The newer techniques are making possible the extension of wage incentives to work for which wage incentive plans were previously considered to be impractical. Work measurement as used in developing wage incentives, further contributes to effective managerial control in many other areas. (See Appendix D.)

In recent years, however, there has been some dissatisfaction with the operation of wage incentive plans. The purpose of this book is to examine the reason for dissatisfaction and outline policies and procedures for avoiding the problems that have been encountered. Ways and means of revitalizing outmoded plans also are discussed. To the extent that we can prevent their deterioration, wage incentive plans will make significant contributions toward lower costs, increased output, and higher real wages. When they are properly designed and administered, they can make significant contributions in maintaining profit margins even when price levels are inflexible. That, in the long run, is the only means of advancing our national economic standards.

Basic Wage Plans

There is no such thing as a perfect pay plan in operation today, and the possibility that one will ever be developed is very remote. Of the two basic types of wage plans, the oldest is based on payment for attendance and is therefore called *daywork*. The other is based on some measure of performance or output and was therefore originally known as piecework; it is more properly called *incentive pay.* The proponents of these plans have been debating the relative merits of the plans for years. Some of the arguments are based on theoretical considerations; others are based on experience. This much is certain: so many factors contribute to the success or failure of any wage plan that a claim of superior merit is valueless without a careful analysis of all of the factors that influence the particular operation.

In a favorable environment—good supervision, excellent management, favorable personnel relations, good employee motivation—high levels of output may result with no incentive plan at all. Contrariwise, the frequent result of an outmoded incentive plan, poor control of labor and labor reporting, and supervisory apathy toward wage incentives is the payment of incentive wages for daywork performance or less. The uninformed or untrained observer may then argue that wage incentives are ineffective and costly and lead to many administrative problems. That is simply not true. The success or failure of any type of wage plan—be it daywork or incentive—depends more on administration and enforcement of good management principles relating to the plan than it does on the technical aspects of the plan itself.

RESTRICTIONS ON INCENTIVES

Most people with an industrial background agree that the properly engineered application of wage incentives, involving a complete program of methods improvement, standardization, and measurement and followed by application of proper incentives, generally reduces costs from 50 to 70 percent of former levels and brings about a corresponding increase in output. Thus we have a paradoxical situation: initially wage incentives reduce cost, greatly improve output, and improve employee earnings and then, after the plan has been in effect for a period of years, cause dissatisfactions.

Early experiences with incentives—generally piecework—led to considerable employee dissatisfaction with their use. Much of the dissatisfaction was caused by indiscriminate rate cutting by shop supervisors. In many cases piece rates were arbitrarily reduced merely because earning levels were unexpectedly high. The natural reaction of the employees was to limit production to just below the assumed level at which rates would again be adjusted. Some of that earlier distrust of incentives persists today. There have been enough instances of rate reduction by one or another type of subterfuge on the part of a few management people to make the attitude understandable.

Because of these abuses, much of the early development of time study techniques and incentive applications conducted by Taylor, Gantt, and others was carried out in a hostile environment. As a result, there was considerable emphasis on selling the wage incentive plan and guaranteeing against any reduction in standards except when there were major changes in methods. The philosophy of no rate cutting except for that reason exists today. It is responsible for a clause in most union contracts stipulating that rates will not be reduced except for changes in methods, tooling, and materials and will be restricted to the elements affected. In many cases it has obstructed improvement of standards.

The restrictive clauses are responsible for extreme rigidity in the standards structure and confine adjustments to the standards to a narrow range of demonstrable changes in operation. In addition, the expressed philosophies of most of the texts on work measurement are limited to development of the best practical method and a careful time study with emphasis on proper leveling. There is almost no discussion of techniques of audit or administration.

Effect of Methods Changes

Wage incentive policies were developed against a background of relatively stable manufacturing with relatively few process changes. Today we are in an era of rapid and frequent changes in design and increasingly rapid technological improvement. Fortunately, obsolescence of the part or product frequently makes the standard obsolete.

It is of utmost importance to note that differences in method have more effect on the rate of accomplishment than variations in work pace. Of the total savings to be realized by the full industrial engineering program of methods-measurement-incentives, approximately 50 percent is the result of methods improvement and standardization. Also, the administrative costs of the methods improvement function are relatively low. The remaining savings can be attributed to the measurement function and to the subsequent application of incentives. Work measurement and incentives bear the highest proportion of administrative costs, but they usually provide the assurance that prescribed methods will be followed in actual practice.

One of the basic arguments of the proponents of measured daywork is based on the contention that the benefits of methods improvement accrue to the company without the administrative costs and headaches of the incentive program. However, the measured daywork plan seldom derives the same increase in productivity as the complete methods-measurement-incentive program. The relative performance levels will be discussed in connection with the various wage incentive plans.

OBSOLESCENCE OF STANDARDS

In an industry characterized by rapid changes in both product and technology, the climate is one of continual improvement in methods, products, facilities, tooling and equipment, and supporting services. Many improvements create obvious changes in manufacturing methods, so that the inapplicability or obsolescence of the rate is recognized by everyone and there is no problem in establishing a new standard.

However, other changes that contribute to the obsolescence of standards are not as easily recognized and are seldom measurable except by audit. These changes, known as creeping changes, may affect either the direct elements of an operation or some of the indirect elements such as allowances for various reasons. For example, an improved stamping die in one end of the factory may produce a part that is held to closer tolerances than those of the original part. This change, in turn, may influence the time for final assembly of the product because less time is spent in fitting and adjusting. A change of this nature might be difficult to justify as a methods change. Furthermore, the chance that the improvement will be reported to the standards department is slight. In fact, by itself, the improvement might very well be minor.

Also, substantial increases in production or equivalent reductions in time required may result from improvements in factory service and support functions. Improved material handling and production scheduling often reduce the time needed for locating the materials for use in the next operation. Improved quality control may result in less time being required for minor repairs and adjustments.

Creeping changes are almost impossible to define, and in most cases they defy any quantitative adjustment to standards by the use of conventional time study procedures. However, the cumulative impact of these changes is a major factor in the obsolescence of wage incentive plans regardless of how carefully the plans may have been devised and installed. Most conventional time studies represent only one point in a continuum of change. It is significant that very few industrial organizations have anything more than a loose and inadequate system for reporting, measuring, and recording changes as they occur.

Many industries are saddled with incentive policies, union contracts, and top management philosophies that have tended to produce a rigid rate structure in the face of continual change in manufacturing methods. Unfortunately, many top-level managers are basically unaware of that relationship. They will express extreme concern about increasing costs, rate grievances, unreasonable union attitudes, ceilings on production, and irregular earnings. They tend to blame the incentive plan or assume that the people responsible for rates are not capable of setting proper ones.

Work measurement methods have improved materially since 1950. Most reasonably well trained industrial engineers can develop standards that will be consistent within acceptable statistical confidence levels. The newer techniques relating to motion study, work sampling, and standard data development, as well as systems of predetermined times such as methods-time measurement and work factor, operate to develop better consistency and accuracy of measurement.

INCENTIVE PLAN OBSOLESCENCE

Evaluation and audit of industrial engineering functions has shown that when an incentive plan has been in effect for ten years or longer, it is usually outmoded. A number of symptoms then appear: performance levels are low, much time is wasted, no action is taken to eliminate unnecessary downtime, workers quit early to clean up, and work actually starts 30 minutes after the beginning of the shift. These shortcomings are invariably due to a lack of maintenance of the system. Necessary revisions have not been made, and existing standards no longer reflect the exact methods in use. Often the standards people are required to operate within the restraints of an outmoded system, and they therefore routinely rebuild old flaws into new standards.

What often happens is that a well-conceived, carefully studied and installed plan developed by well-trained engineers is turned over to a small group of relatively untrained time study men with little policy or technical direction from management.[1] Here is a representative instance. Several years ago, a series of independent time studies on a sampling basis were made in several departments of a rather large plant. The studies were to be used in preparation for an arbitration case involving a number of standards that were being disputed by the union.

[1] Glenn D. Wolfe, "Wage Incentives: Prairie Schooner on the Expressway?" *Industrial Management* (April 1966).

The results of the time studies, even with the most liberal treatment, developed standards that averaged about 75 percent of the time values then in effect. In other words, the standards were about 33 percent loose yet those very same standards were being grieved by the union as too tight. However, the reaction of management to the developments was one of elation at the probable outcome of the arbitration hearing rather than concern over the evidence that the incentive structure was completely outmoded.

Far too many top management people are anxious to accept any new wage incentive plan or new method of measurement as the solution to their wage incentive problems or as the means of correcting an outmoded plan. Unfortunately, they are often extremely reluctant to take the action necessary to eliminate the causes for the deterioration of their present plans. Problems such as poor timekeeping, neglect of auditing, and the developing of proper supervisory attitudes toward the incentive plan are frequently brushed aside. But unless those problems are corrected, any new plan is destined to suffer the fate of its predecessor.

REQUISITES FOR PLAN SUCCESS

To be successful, a wage incentive plan must have the following characteristics:

1. *The plan should permit earnings above the base rate.* A rate structure that pays only a low percent of gain for good incentive performance simply is lacking in incentive appeal. Good incentive performance (high task) should produce incentive gains of at least 30 percent. There is a substantial trend of opinion today that even 30 percent is insufficient and that the ideal gains for high task performance (median incentive pace) should approximate 35 percent.

2. *The plan should benefit both the company and the individual; that is, it should increase employee earnings and reduce company costs.* The plan should require performance above normal daywork levels. Also, the cost of administering the plan must be minimal and should not outweigh the potential cost savings.

3. *The plan should be simple and understandable.* Lack of understandability has resulted in the abandonment of many otherwise well-planned systems. Careful indoctrination of the workers is important. The operator should, if possible, be able to figure his own pay from his daily production. That is obviously difficult to do in large group installations, but in general the plan with the simplest mathematics has the best chance of acceptance by employees.

4. *Standards must be protected from capricious and indiscriminate rate cutting.* Here policy must recognize the difference between the performance of an unusually skilled operator using a standard method and that of a normal operator using an improved method. Basic to this policy is the doctrine that method determines time. Operator ingenuity in devising improved methods must be encouraged and rewarded. The reward, however, must be separate from the incentive structure, and the incentive structure must be revised promptly to reflect the improved method regardless of its origin.

5. *Earnings should not be affected by factors beyond the control of the operator.* The operator must be given day rate for delays due to improper tooling, poor materials, lack of materials, and other factors beyond the normal delays that are included in the averaging of his incentive. Wide variations of either materials or process are inherent in many operations. Such situations require careful averaging and the spelling out of acceptable limits of variations. Variations beyond those limits should then be adjusted for.

Reasons for Plan Failure

The failure of incentive plans has been found[2] to be attributable to fundamental deficiencies in the plan (41.5 percent), inept human relations (32.5 percent), or poor technical administration (26 percent). Fundamental deficiencies include poor standards, low incentive coverage of direct productive work, a ceiling on earnings, no indirect incentives, no supervisory incentives, and a complicated pay formula.

Inept human relations result from insufficient supervisory training, absence of a guarantee of standards, failure to require a fair day's work, negotiation of standards with the union, failure to understand the plan, lack of top management support, and poor training of operators.

Poor technical administration includes the following: Methods changes are not coordinated with standards revisions; base rates are faulty; grievance procedures result in negotiated changes, large groups on incentive, poor production planning, and poor quality control.

Need for Top Management Support

A broad basic policy covering the wage incentive plan and the acceptance of the plan on all administrative levels are vital to success-

---

[2] Benjamin W. Niebel, *Motion and Time Study*, 4th Ed. (Homewood, Ill.: Richard D. Irwin, Inc., 1967), p. 557. The data were secured in a survey by Bruce Payne of Bruce Payne and Associates, Inc.

ful plan operation. The policy should outline the company's basic philosophy regarding wage incentives, conditions under which incentives will be applied, the ways in which incentives will be controlled and administered, the designation of responsibility for devising, controlling, and reporting changes in methods, and the manner in which the entire incentive system will be maintained and audited. The policy must be put in writing and made available to all those affected—union as well as company.

Appendix A is an example of such a wage incentive policy. It should, of course, be taken only as a general approach; for example, ultimate responsibility for methods will differ with the individual concern.

The mere development and distribution of a policy such as the one reproduced in Appendix A is not sufficient to insure proper application of the policy. Management must accept the responsibility not only for developing the program but for enforcing it. That means that the entire content of the policy must be reviewed by all departments and groups concerned: personnel, standards, accounting, shop supervision and such of its supporting functions as quality control, and the union representatives. The development and application of a policy concerning wage incentives is subject to any existent collective bargaining agreement with a union. If there is such an agreement, the policy cannot be developed and issued unilaterally but must be discussed with the proper union representatives.

NEED FOR CAPABLE ADMINISTRATION

It is essential that any work measurement or incentive program be administered by a dedicated, capable, and fair-minded individual who knows and adheres to the fundamental principles of the established program. It is equally essential that the basic principles of the plan receive adequate top management support both in dealings with the union in grievance procedures relating to standards and in seeing to it that the plan is adequately administered by shop supervisors as well as the timekeeping organization. An incentive system is much like a complicated machine, and in the hands of anyone who is not thoroughly trained in its intricacies, it usually becomes a malfunctioning piece of equipment. Every departure from fundamental rules or policies in the early history of an incentive plan can—and usually does—develop into disastrous deviations with the passage of time.

2

Wage Incentive Plans

INCENTIVE PAY ARRANGEMENTS vary from simple piecework systems to complicated profit-sharing plans. Which plan is selected depends to a great extent on management policy and the need for minimum unit labor costs. However, the numerous plans do have varying degrees of suitability or adaptability to the kind of work being performed. In this chapter the main features of the following representative incentive plans will be discussed:

Measured daywork:
    Non-incentive
    With merit rating
Piecework
Time payment plans:
    Straight-line (standard-hour)
    Sharing
Indirect plans:
    Scanlon
    Rucker
    Profit-sharing
    Incentive management
    Cost ratio
Multifactor plans
Incentives for indirect operations
Supervisory incentives

There are many other incentive plans in use, but most of them are essentially the basic plans with modifications to accomplish some particular effects on earnings at various performance levels. In a later chapter the suitability of the various incentive plans will be related to the basic types of work being performed.

ADVANTAGES AND DISADVANTAGES OF DAYWORK

Most incentive plans start with daywork as a base from which additional earnings are derived through increased production. That is also the method of payment for non-incentive operations. Therefore, a short discussion of the advantages and disadvantages of the daywork plan must precede a more thorough discussion of current wage incentive plans.

Daywork is still the conventional method of wage payment where measurement of output is impractical for one reason or another or where management policy is against the use of incentives. It has the underlying advantages that it is simple and that the employee knows exactly what his earnings will be for a given period of time. Payroll calculations are simple. Methods improvements and technological changes are easier to introduce than under incentive systems, where such changes are usually accompanied by a reduction in incentive rates. However, there is also less assurance that the new methods will be followed.

Most industry was started on the principle that the supervisor is the sole judge of a satisfactory day's output for the employee. Under daywork, motivation is often negative. A reprimand or discharge may be forthcoming in the event that the day's production is not satisfactory to the supervisor. Motivation toward superior performance is largely lacking because there is no tangible relationship between superior performance and increased wages. Productivity under daywork varies widely and frequently depends on the abilities of the individual supervisor, on employee morale in the plant and, for the individual, on a socially accepted level of performance in a given location.

Productivity levels vary widely from plant to plant, but it is generally conceded that under daywork they are approximately 50 to 60 percent of those attainable by good incentive application. Thus, in general, daywork requires more effective supervision than that required under incentive plans to attain satisfactory rates of output. Also, levels of output are unpredictable, which makes it extremely difficult to quote on new work or to schedule production. Because of the wide fluctuations in levels of output, standard costs are quite impractical and job costs based on factory records may be highly unreliable.

The unsatisfactory conditions surrounding daywork have led to the development of the many incentive plans designed to increase productivity and eliminate the disadvantages of daywork.

Measured Daywork

There are two plans for compensating for measured daywork: *non-incentive,* under which records of the employee's performance are kept but there is no adjustment to pay scales as a result of performance, and *with merit rating,* under which the employee's performance is used to make adjustments in the base wage.

NON-INCENTIVE MEASURED DAYWORK

Under the non-incentive measured daywork plan, the employee's output is recorded against established standards (time study, past performance, or even an estimate of the time required to do the work) but there is no relation between an employee's performance and his earnings. However, the fact that his performance is being measured against some standard is expected to encourage the employee to equal or better his work quota. Conversely, the employee may expect questioning or criticism if his performance falls below accepted levels.

Advantages. Since the employee knows that his output is being compared with quotas, there is some challenge to meet the quotas. As agreement between expected output and actual output improves, the plan begins to facilitate improved production control as well as the collection of more reliable cost data. This, in turn, brings about the development of rough standard costs and greatly assists pricing and quoting procedures.

Disadvantages. More formalized work measurement introduces many of the administrative costs of a complete incentive installation. Since the work measurement function is by far the largest cost element in a methods-measurement-incentive program, measured daywork incurs high administrative and engineering expense with no assurance that attainable production levels will be achieved. Actual production attainment depends to a very great extent on the strength and effectiveness of the supervisory staff.

MEASURED DAYWORK WITH MERIT RATING

Measured daywork with merit rating involves a periodic review and evaluation of the individual employee's performance against established criteria such as productive output, quality, and attendance. The employee's base wage is then adjusted, usually within prescribed limits, and the adjusted wage is in effect during the next review period. Merit reviews are usually made regularly, often at intervals of three to six months.

In another version of the plan, the employee's wage may be adjusted in direct proportion to his performance against the standard. Usually, under such a plan, the reviews are made at more frequent intervals.

Advantages. The employee's productive output in terms of his performance against standards is emphasized to a greater degree than under non-incentive measured daywork. The assumption is that an employee will achieve and maintain his best performance regardless of where he works or what type of work he is required to do and that he will seek to maintain that level of performance in order to achieve his maximum base wage. Management derives some improvement in control over performance; cost estimates become more reliable; and production scheduling becomes more realistic.

Disadvantages. Usually the range of adjustment to the base pay through merit rating procedures operates in a fairly restricted series of levels, generally plus or minus about 10 percent from the occupational base wage. As a result, there is little incentive toward productive output beyond what is necessary to continue at the maximum base wage for a given occupation. Consequently, performance in industries using measured daywork with merit ratings falls about halfway between that attainable by unmeasured daywork and that attainable by well-planned and well-administered conventional incentive. It is argued by its proponents that measured daywork eliminates many of the problems of obsolescence and rate grievances common to the conventional incentive system, but the problem of obsolescence of standards remains the same regardless of whether a daywork or an incentive plan is in use. Also, there is much less pressure to maintain standards.

As the range of wage adjustments attainable under merit reviews becomes greater, the plan approaches some of the characteristics of a conventional incentive system. This, in turn, leads to a greater number of grievances concerning allegedly tight standards.

Piecework

Piecework is defined as direct payment for production in terms of monetary units. It is probably the oldest of all incentive systems, and for that reason the term "piecework" has often been loosely and incorrectly applied to other types of incentive plans. Early piece rates were based on either estimates or individual bargaining. They were generally determined by relating expected output to some level of earnings above the employee's daywork wage, the exact amount being determined by management policy. However, piece rates can be established from time studies in the same manner as other types of incentives.

Advantages. The primary advantage of piecework is simplicity. The employee knows exactly what his pay will be. Also, reward is directly proportional to effort.

Disadvantages. As a result of several disadvantages of the system, relatively few industrial installations use piecework. The disadvantages are:

1. For production scheduling, monetary piece rates must be converted to expected unit times by relating the piecework rate to the proper base wage. Since the unit time may be a variable or, in some cases, even unknown, the results are undependable and also require additional computations.

2. Under piecework there is no provision for recognizing any factor other than production. Versatility, length of service, or dependability cannot be considered in the plan.

3. Under prevailing conditions of wage negotiations with frequent increases in the wage structure, the maintenance of a piece rate system becomes incredibly difficult. A change in the basic wage structure usually requires the recomputation of thousands of individual piece rates. This difficulty, together with the need for constant revision, has been the greatest factor contributing to the decline in the use of the piecework incentive.

4. Because of the rather loose basis of evaluation that is typical of many piece rate plans, the adjustment of the rate for methods changes, either up or down, becomes exceedingly difficult. Although the problem is reduced when conventional time study methods are used, it seldom disappears.

Time Payment Plans

Under time payment plans, payment is expressed in units of time. Standards are usually expressed in hours or decimal hours per unit of production, and time so earned is paid for at the employee's occupational wage.

Advantages. The major factors that influence the use of time payment plans are as follows:

1. Payment is based on time rather than money. Since time is generated by method, there is a closer and more obvious relationship between the standard and the operation content.

2. Changes in the wage structure merely require changes in the payroll multipliers and do not alter the time-based incentive standards.

3. It is possible to develop personal rates within each occupational group to provide for such factors as length of service, skill, and dependability.

4. A more objective study of productivity is possible: incentive gains are based on the ratio of earned hours to actual hours. A comparable measurement is quite difficult under piece rates. Discussions of productivity in terms of time rather than dollar earnings have a more objective outlook.

5. The evaluation of performance in terms of standard hours earned divided by actual hours of input forms an excellent basis for comparing performance of individuals, departments, and total factory operations.

6. When standards are related to time, production scheduling becomes more meaningful.

STRAIGHT-LINE (STANDARD-HOUR) PLANS

Under a straight-line, or standard-hour, plan, payment is in direct proportion to output, and therefore this type of plan is often characterized as a 100 percent or 1:1 plan.

Advantages. The simplicity of the plan promotes good employee acceptance. Other advantages, which have resulted in widespread adoption, are simplicity in payroll computations, adaptability to production scheduling, and usefulness in evaluating performance of individuals, departments, and plants on a variety of operations.

Disadvantages. Because standard-hour plans are widely used and accepted, they have sometimes been used in situations to which they are not well suited. When conditions or operations have not been well standardized or when fluctuations in materials or methods require a high degree of averaging, the result is a wide fluctuation in incentive earnings. The frequent consequences are serious personnel and administrative problems.

In the following example, rates and earnings are computed for the same set of assumed conditions under both the piecework and standard-hour plans.

EXAMPLE. The basic assumptions are as follows:

Daywork wage $2.00 per hour
Estimated (or studied) production
    at incentive pace   150 pieces per hour
Policy for median incentive earnings   25% gain over day rate

Therefore, under the piecework plan:

$2.00 + ($2.00 \times 25\%) = $2.50 = 150$ pieces

$$\text{Standard rate} = \frac{\$2.50 \times 100}{150} = \$1.67 \text{ per 100 pieces}$$

Assume that the operator produces 1250 pieces in 8 hours; then

1250 at $1.67 per 100 = $20.80 daily pay
Daywork rate for 8 hours = 2.00×8 hours = $16.00
Incentive gain = $20.80 \div $16.00 \times 100 = 130\%$

Under the standard-hour plan, with the same assumptions,

150 pieces = 1 hour + (1 hour $\times$ 25%) = 1.25 hours
1.25 hours $\div$ 150 piece = .00833 hour per piece
Standard rate = .833 hour per 100 pieces

As before, assume that the operator produces 1250 pieces in 8 hours; then

$1250 \times .833 = 10.4$ earned hours
$10.4 \times 2.00 per hour = $20.80 daily pay
Incentive gain = $10.4 \div 8 \times 100 = 130\%$

So that the incentive earnings are the same percent of daywork pay as under the piecework plan.

SHARING PLANS

Most sharing plans are calculated on a time basis similar to that of the standard-hour plan. The fundamental difference is that the time saved by incentive effort is only partially credited to the operator. In the Halsey 50-50 plan—one of the more common applications of the type—the operator receives one-half of the savings. In other modifications, the operator might receive two-thirds of the savings and management one-third or the other way around.

The distribution may also be calculated and distributed on a per-

cent basis as in the Rowan plan. Here the savings in time are calculated as a percent of the standard time allowed. The percent is then
added to the actual time of the operator. The methods of calculation
for a given set of circumstances under the Halsey 50-50 and the
Rowan plans are illustrated in the following example.

EXAMPLE. The basic assumptions are as follows:

Standard time for task   10 hours
Actual time for task   7 hours

Under the Halsey 50-50 plan:

Standard time	10.0 hours
Actual time	7.0 hours
Time saved	3.0 hours
50% of savings	1.5 hours
Operator's pay at his occupational rate	7.0 hours + 1.5 hours = 8.5 hours

Incentive gain = $8.5 \div 7 \times 100 = 122\%$
Performance = $10 \div 7 \times 100 = 143\%$

Under the Rowan plan:

Standard time	10.0 hours
Actual time	7.0 hours
Time saved	3.0 hours
Percent saved	$3.0 \div 10.0 \times 100 = 30\%$
Operator's share of savings	$30\% \times 7.0$ hours = 2.1 hours
Operator's pay at his occupational rate	7.0 hours + 2.1 hours = 9.1 hours

Incentive gain = $9.1 \div 7.0 \times 100 = 130\%$
Performance = $10 \div 7 \times 100 = 143\%$

The incentive gain calculated by this formula always equals the percent
of standard time saved by the operator.

The Bedaux Plan is basically a Halsey sharing plan that gives
75 percent of the time saved to the operator and the remaining 25
percent to foremen, servicemen, and other indirect shop personnel,
who will therefore presumably intensify their support of the direct
work.

One fundamental characteristic of all sharing plans is that the
superior operators do not receive as high a level of incentive gains
as they would under the standard-hour plan and, conversely, the
substandard operators begin to derive some incentive earnings at

lower levels of performance. The performance-earnings curve is much flatter.

Advantages. All sharing plans have these advantages in common:

1. When work has not been well standardized or when there are considerable process or material variations to be absorbed, sharing plans reduce the extreme fluctuations in earnings that are characteristic of the straight-line plans.

2. A sharing plan is easy to introduce in a shop where no incentives have previously been used, since incentive gains begin at a lower level of performance (often equivalent to daywork) and initial incentive performance levels do not differ too widely from operator concepts of daywork performance.

3. The rather flat performance-earnings curve makes the earning levels less vulnerable to methods or process improvement. This in turn makes the sharing plan acceptable where it is impractical to expect too much attention to standards maintenance or where normal process or material variations require a high degree of averaging.

Disadvantages. These disadvantages also are common to all sharing plans:

1. The incentive is weaker and there is not the strong inducement for the superior operator to achieve maximum incentive effort.

2. There are occasional objections to the sharing feature. Some people wonder why they should "split with the company."

3. Payroll calculations are somewhat more complicated than under the straight-line plans.

General remarks on sharing plans. Figure 1 shows a graph of incentive gains at various levels of performance under the standard-hour, Halsey 50-50, and Rowan plans. In order to permit useful comparisons, the basic figures were designed to develop median earned incentive gains at 125 percent of day rate at high task level or 125 percent relative performance. Under the standard-hour plan incentive gains begin at normal task performance and increase by 1 percent for each 1 percent of additional performance.

Under the Halsey 50-50 plan, incentive gains begin at the usual range of daywork performance (low task) and are approximately 115 percent of day rate at the normal task level and equal to the standard-hour plan rate at high task level (125 percent of relative performance) but increase more slowly beyond that point. This illustrates the statement made earlier that incentive gains begin at a much lower level of performance than they do under the standard-hour plan but that superior performers gain less than they would under the standard-hour plan.

Figure 1. Incentive gains at various performance levels.

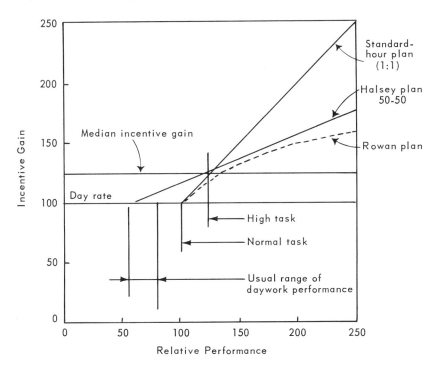

Incentive gains under the Rowan plan begin at normal task level, are comparable with earnings under the Halsey plan at approximately 160 to 185 percent of relative performance, but diminish slightly beyond that point. The construction of the Rowan formula is such that it is mathematically impossible to exceed 200 percent incentive gain, even with infinite relative performance (zero actual time).

A plan that has many of the desirable characteristics of sharing plans was developed in 1963 by Kearney & Trecker Corporation, a West Allis, Wisconsin, builder of machine tools, in collaboration with its union and is called the earnings sharing plan (ESP).[1] It permits broad averaging of process variables. Another feature is the lengthy computation period, which has a desirable effect in stabilizing employee earnings. It was planned as a replacement for an earlier standard-hour plan that had become unworkable in a number of areas

[1] Thanks are due Kearney & Trecker Corporation for supplying the information on ESP and permitting its use here.

because of changes in product mix, shorter runs, and increasing difficulties in maintaining adequate rate coverage.

Originally intended for use in assembly and machine erection areas, ESP has been successfully extended to numerous other departments. The plan uses condensed standard data collected from a base of existing records, as well as conventional time studies, to set incentive rates on a variety of operations. There are three types of rates:

1. Regular rates for operations that normally repeat in subsequent lots.
2. One-lot rates for operations that are not expected to repeat or that will be revised for the next lot.
3. Estimated rates for operations such that the setting of rates by other means is not practical: experimental work, one-lot runs, and similar operations.

These rates are calculated to produce median incentive gains of 120 percent for the average operator after the 50-50 split for production over 100 percent. One feature of the rates is that they do not include the conventional delay allowances, which are studied separately for each work center and are applied to the attendance hours on rated work. They do include such factors as personal time, fatigue, fitting for assembly, crane delays, tool trouble, and time spent in obtaining tools. Punching out for delays is limited to machine breakdown, no work available, time spent in medical department, meetings of union representatives with the company, time spent in processing complaints and grievances in the grievance procedure, and company-sponsored meetings during working hours.

The computation for one individual job is illustrated by the following example.

EXAMPLE. The basic assumptions are:

ESP rate   1.0 hour per piece
Work center delay allowance   20%
Operator production   10 pieces in 7.5 hours
Produced hours = 10 pieces × 1.0 hour per piece + (20% × 7.5 hours)
               = 11.5 hours

Earned hours for all work done during the four-week computation period are calculated and added to non-incentive hours. The pay calculation is then made in the following manner:

Bonus over base (in percent)

$$= \frac{\text{total produced hours} - \text{actual hours on ESP}}{\text{actual hours on ESP}} \times \frac{1}{2} \times 100$$

Thus if the operator over a four-week period accumulated a total of 180 hours produced in 130 actual hours, his bonus over base would be

$$\frac{180 - 130}{130} \times \frac{1}{2} \times 100 = 19.2\%$$

Assume that during the same four-week period a worker also had 20 hours of non-incentive work for a total of 150 attendance hours. His productivity rate, to be used as a multiplier in connection with his base wage, would then be

$$\frac{119.2\% \times 130 \text{ hours} + 20 \text{ hours (non-incentive)}}{150 \text{ total actual hours}} = \frac{155 + 20}{150} \times 100 = 116.6\%$$

During the next four weeks, the productivity rate as established would be multiplied by the occupational wage in order to calculate the worker's weekly pay. During the same four-week pay period the employee would be developing a new productivity rate for use in the subsequent four-week period.

In the preceding example the ESP has been simplified somewhat by omission of irrelevant details. The plan has functioned quite well in an environment in which maintaining a conventional standard-hour or Halsey plan would be difficult, if not impractical, because of the variety of work and the short runs.

Indirect Plans

Indirect incentives are so called because measurement is based not on detailed inputs (pieces or operations completed in some standard time value), but rather on total input of labor (departmental or plantwide) related to outputs in terms of completed product, dollars of shipments, or similar criteria. Indirect incentives should not be confused with incentives for indirect labor, a subject that will be discussed later.

Indirect incentives are generally based on some cost or productivity formula and are applied on a departmental or plantwide basis. Their strongest appeal is to the management that has a philosophy of developing teamwork and encouraging constructive thinking by employees and is willing to discuss its plans and the results of its operations with its employees or their representatives. Management must also be objective enough to discuss mutual problems and all relevant data with employee groups and be willing to entertain occasional criticism and constructive suggestions. It is definitely an approach to Professor McGregor's theory Y.[2] Generally speaking, such plans have had their greatest success when the following factors were present:

- Relatively small employee groups—about 300 maximum.
- Well-defined product line without major variations in cost-price ratios.
- Highly competent supervision.
- Mutual respect between management and labor.
- Great interest and participation in the plan by top management.
- A willingness on the part of top management to sit down with employees or their representatives and discuss the periodic results of operations, whether good or bad.

Advantages. Plantwide indirect incentive plans have certain advantages. Under proper environmental conditions and with mutual confidence between labor and management, they can be a strong influence toward group dynamics, cooperative efforts, and the development of individual contributions to the success of the enterprise as a whole. They have the additional advantage that every employee can be covered by incentives. That is an improvement over customary incentives based on direct measurement, which are usually limited to measurable productive operations and are rarely applied to factory indirect labor. Thus, the indirect plans result in 100 percent incentive coverage in the plant rather than the 60 to 80 percent coverage of direct operations only that is characteristic of most conventional plans.

Disadvantages. Offsetting the advantages, however, is the fact that performance levels under indirect incentive plans are usually not as high as those under strong individual incentive plans. Plantwide incentives are also susceptible to failure for reason of such external conditions as major changes in markets or in the economic climate.

[2] Douglas McGregor, "The Human Side of Enterprise," *Management Review* (November, 1957). Mr. McGregor states that under theory Y, "The essential task of management is to arrange organizational conditions and methods of operation so that people can achieve their own goals best by directing their own efforts toward organizational objectives."

Nor can these plans be installed and then forgotten. Administrative costs of plantwide plans are very moderate, but continual maintenance and study are required to prevent their obsolescence. Much of their continuing success lies in management's ability to keep employees interested in the plan after its initial inception. This usually requires periodic meetings of management and employee representatives to discuss operating results, point out future developments that may have a positive or negative effect on the plan, and encourage worthwhile suggestions from employees.

THE SCANLON PLAN

The Scanlon plan is a pioneer union-management productivity plan that is based heavily on union-management cooperation. It was developed by Joseph Scanlon, a union officer on the Steelworkers' Organizing Committee, and the Pittsburgh Steel Company which was having economic difficulties at that time. Although the plan had as its primary aim the survival of the company, it significantly reduced operating costs with resulting profitability to the company and increased earnings to the workers. Much of the philosophy of the Scanlon plan is based on building a working relationship between management and labor that will enable the two to become a single team devoted to increased productivity.

Under the plan, the first step is to develop a normal labor cost for the plant under consideration. The normal labor cost is preferably based on or related to some significant measurement of gross output such as tons of steel produced or number of units shipped. Historical ratios of labor cost per unit of output are established, usually subject to agreement with the union. Savings derived from the program are distributed to labor. The benefits accruing to management are considered to be those of increased sales and increased profits due to greater output relative to plant overhead. In other words, the theory is that labor should profit from improved performance and the company should profit from a better use of its assets. Provisions are usually made for negotiating changes in the formula necessitated by a change in conditions, as by the introduction of major units of capital equipment designed to reduce labor costs or a major change in the cost-price relationship of the product.

Under the Scanlon plan, the emphasis is less on measurement of labor content than on negotiating the normal proportion of labor. The plan requires mutual confidence between labor and management and collective bargaining of a high order. A major feature of the plan is the use of production committees whose function it is to review suggestions on how time and effort can be saved. These committees are empowered to put into effect any suggestions that do not involve other departments or expenditures for capital equipment. The activities of the production committees are supervised by a screening committee composed of representatives of management and labor from various departments. In addition to supervising the operation of the production committees, the screening committee rules on suggestions that involve several departments or require major capital expenditures.

The Scanlon plan had some popularity during the late 1940s and early 1950s, but there are relatively few such installations at the present time.

THE RUCKER PLAN

The Rucker plan, also known as a share-of-production plan, is based on value added by manufacture. As in the Scanlon plan, formulas are generally established from historical records. The value added by manufacture is usually determined by period sales (adjusted to work in process and inventory variations) less the cost of materials used. Labor's share of the value added by manufacture is, again, historically determined as a percent of the value added, and it usually includes all labor, whether direct or indirect. Labor-controlled items such as supplies, scrap, rework, and maintenance may also be included. Periodic savings over these historic values are then returned to the employees on some agreed-on basis, often 50 percent. One very interesting feature of the Rucker plan that should be of considerable interest to management is that any negotiated wage increases that cannot be matched by either increased productivity or compensating price increases immediately affect the performance ratios of the Rucker plan. They will, in fact, show up almost immediately in reduced earnings under such a plan. This demonstrates unmistakably the direct relationship between productivity and real wages. The following is an actual example.

Gross sales for month		$958,000
Net change; work in process		20,000
Total product manufactured and on hand		$978,000
Materials used	$597,000	
Customer service and adjustments	8,000	
Total purchases and adjustments		605,000
Value added by manufacture		$373,000

Labor's share of value added
(30% of value added by manufacture is used as
historical standard in this example.) $112,000
Actual cost of value added
(from accounting records)   98,000
Gross savings by joint effort $ 14,000
Employees' share of savings (50%) $ 7,000

Note: Labor's share of value added and actual cost of value added include all hourly labor, overtime, shift premiums, and other fringe benefits as well as shop supplies, maintenance, tools, and repairs. Values are assumed.

One of the prominent features of the Scanlon plan is negotiation of labor ratios; under the Rucker plan, this determination is largely based on past accounting records and is not usually considered as freely bargainable. The Rucker plan has the advantage of offering incentives for savings not only in labor but also in material, scrap, rework, and use of shop supplies. Any savings in those items goes into the fund for employee distribution. That makes the plan particularly advantageous where there is a high proportion of material cost and employee attention to quality factors can therefore effect substantial cost savings. As in the Scanlon plan, the Rucker plan is best suited to the small or medium-sized company with a well-defined product line, uniform labor content throughout the mix, mutual respect and confidence between labor and management, and good supervision. Labor participation in the form of labor-management committees to review operating results and discuss any unusual features of past operations is also essential.

PROFIT-SHARING PLANS

Profit sharing, in the opinion of most industrial engineers, is not an incentive plan; certainly it is a weak inducement to maximum daily performance. It has certain appeals to those who are interested in group dynamics and to proponents of profit sharing as a social device. It is based on the premise that people can be influenced to produce more effectively, conserve supplies and materials, and cooperate with management in improving methods and in introducing improved processes if they are assured of participating in the benefits derived therefrom.

There is some validity to that argument. The problem is that profits are affected by many factors beyond the control of the employees. Astute purchasing policies, the fortuitous introduction of a new product at just the right time, and generally rising market demands can frequently enhance profits even in the face of declining manufacturing effectiveness. A reversal of the same factors can frequently wipe out profits in spite of exceptional performance by all employees. Thus, profit sharing frequently violates the basic principle of wage incentives, which is that the reward should be proportional to performance.

When profits are distributed on some basis at the end of the year—frequently as a contribution to an employee's pension and retirement fund—there is no question that goodwill is created and employee turnover should decrease. Profit-sharing plans are particularly attractive to individuals who have a considerable length of service. However, ill-feeling frequently results when there are no profits to be distributed. Management is often criticized for incompetence under such circumstances, even though the loss in profits may have been due to completely uncontrollable external factors such as unfavorable sales volume or major market changes.

INCENTIVE MANAGEMENT PLAN

James F. Lincoln, of the Lincoln Electric Company of Cleveland, has developed a plantwide incentive system called *incentive management*. In a strict sense, his plan is similar to profit sharing in that company profits, after deductions for nominal dividends and amounts set aside by the directors for future corporate growth, are divided as a bonus among the workers and management. Mr. Lincoln states[3] that this bonus is divided "on the basis of the contribution of each person to the success of the company for the year in question. It has represented a total amount paid to the worker of from approximately 20 percent of wages and salaries per year as a minimum to a maximum of 128 percent per year, over the last 16 years. The average total bonus for each factory worker in that time has exceeded $40,000."

The difference between the success of the Lincoln plan and the more conventional profit-sharing plan is undoubtedly due in a large measure to Mr. Lincoln's personal philosophy and his ability to create active and enthusiastic support for his plan at all levels in the organization. However, the positive factors that contribute to the plan's success are the very strong merit rating review and the definite efforts made to weed out the inferior employee and attract the superior performer.

[3] James F. Lincoln, *Incentive Management* (Cleveland, Ohio: The Lincoln Electric Company, 1951).

The philosophies expressed in Mr. Lincoln's book are directed toward the development of the latent talents of each individual in the organization with great emphasis on cooperative efforts toward cost reduction in all possible areas. The success of the plan is, in all probability, due more to the development of this group philosophy and the particular environmental situation than to the basic arithmetic of the plan itself. The successful history of the plan points out the vital need for top management support in the administration of any wage incentive plan.

COST RATIO PLANS

Cost ratio plans are based on assumed or historical relationships between the cost of the activity being measured and some controlling function such as direct labor dollar values or units of product shipped. For example, analysis of past records might indicate a well-defined relationship between material handling costs and the input of standard labor hours. Similarly, there might be a well-defined relationship between shipping labor and the dollar value of shipments. Incentive payments to material handlers and to shipping room personnel could then be based on improvements in the historical relationships or ratios.

The cost ratio approach is applicable to numerous production-oriented operations such as shipping, receiving, material handling, normal machine maintenance, inspection, and tool repairs, that is, to factory support accounts. However, not all indirect activities are production-related. Janitorial work, sweeping, routine building maintenance, and similar functions do not as a rule vary with production levels. The application of incentives to that type of work may require reference to previous cost records, budgets, or similar sources.

One problem that arises from dependence on past ratios or cost records is that the records have no relationship to the potential for improvement within the activity. For example, an activity that has been well supervised and has attained reasonably good performance levels in the past does not have the same potential for improvement as an activity that has been poorly supervised and has permitted loosely organized work habits among the employees.

One approach that has been used is to study performance by means of work sampling and simultaneous performance rating. Assume that studies indicated that a group of people working on a certain activity were busy 75 percent of the time and that the average of observed performance levels during the period of observation was 80 percent. The conclusion would be that the group was operating at a level of effectiveness of 60 percent (.80 × .75 × 100). That factor could then be used as a reference point in constructing the formula for an incentive based on cost improvement. The mechanics of the plan are illustrated by the following example.

EXAMPLE. A material handling operation involving a group of five fork truck operators historically cost 18 percent of standard direct labor dollars for the division. Also, work samplings indicated an 80 percent utilization of labor and a performance level of 60 percent. That would indicate an overall effectiveness of .80 × .60 × 100 = 48 percent. In other words, the 18 percent ratio was based on an overall effectiveness of 48 percent (which could be rounded to 50 percent).

After reviewing the situation, the industrial engineering staff, with management approval, developed a plan that would begin incentive payments at a 70 percent level of effectiveness and would pay an incentive gain of 125 percent if the effectiveness of the unit increased to 100 percent. The plan was to be based on a calculation period of one week. The basic factors permitted the construction of the accompanying table. The calculations are as follows:

Cost Ratio	Department Effectiveness, Percent	Weekly Bonus, Percent	Cost Ratio	Department Effectiveness, Percent	Weekly Bonus, Percent
18.0	60	0	13.5	80	8
17.5	61	0	13.0	83	11
17.0	63	0	12.5	86	14
16.5	65	0	12.0	90	17
16.0	67	0	11.5	94	20
15.5	69	0	11.0	98	23
15.0	72	2	10.5	102	26
14.5	74	4	10.0	106	30
14.0	77	6			

Standard direct labor weekly payroll	$4750
Actual fork truck operator weekly payroll	$ 570
Materials handling cost ratio, $570 ÷ $4750	12%
Department effectiveness	90% (from table)
Weekly bonus to fork truck operators	17% (from table)
Bonus, 17% × $570	$97

Cost structure:

Base pay of fork truck operators	$570
Bonus, 17% of $570	97
Total labor cost	$667
Historical cost, 18% of $4750	$855
Savings by plan (one week)	$188

A cost ratio plan can be installed with extremely low initial costs for industrial engineering, and the cost of administering the plan is negligible. The values of the factors used must be determined by careful study of existing data, and the bonus percents used are largely based on skilled judgment of the potential for improvement, management policy concerning median incentive gains, and incentive gains in related areas.

As with any other type of incentive, proper controls are vitally necessary. Time spent on the activity must be correctly accounted for, and means for verification of records must be provided. Since the type of activity usually included in cost ratio plans is not adequately planned and the details of the work itself are subject to wide variations, the control of quality and performance becomes a vital factor and can be safeguarded only by competent supervision and frequent intensive evaluation of quality and performance factors by staff personnel not directly involved in the plan itself.

Multifactor Plans

There are some industries and some types of operations in which labor costs are relatively small in comparison with the operating costs of expensive machinery or process equipment. There are other situations in which savings due to improved utilization of material or reduction of scrap or rework are highly significant factors and may outweigh the labor costs involved in the performance of the operation. For example, the hourly operating costs of an expensive numerically controlled machining center might run as high as $50 an hour as compared with labor costs of only $3 an hour. As another example, in tannery operations the value of the hides processed far outweighs the cost of the labor involved.

In work with such cost characteristics, multifactor incentive plans are of considerable benefit. The labor content of the operation can very often be measured by conventional time study procedures. Secondary adjustments can then be made on the basis of machine use, material use, yield of acceptable product, or some other factor to measure required quality. When the industrial trend is toward the introduction of expensive and highly sophisticated equipment and processes, the incentives should be designed to give greatest attention to the lowest unit cost of product: labor *plus* machine overhead *plus* material use.

No general formula is applicable to multifactor plans. Each plan must be developed through a carefully engineered study based on the relative values and controllability of the factors involved. Conventional time study methods are inadequate for such purposes. The following example of a multifactor plan uses the percent defective as a second factor after the usual production incentive. It can be applied to many different types of operations in which material cost is a significant item, and quality is under the operator's control.

EXAMPLE. In a vitreous enameling operation the value of the material at a certain stage is well in excess of the labor cost of the operation. Time studies have developed a production incentive. Subsequent analysis of inspection records has indicated that 5 percent is a reasonably attainable minimum of defectives on the operation. A secondary adjustment to standard hours earned on incentive is developed into the accompanying table.

Actual Percent Defective	Quantity Multiplier	Actual Percent Defective	Quantity Multiplier
0.0	1.10	6.0	.98
1.0	1.08	7.0	.96
2.0	1.06	8.0	.94
3.0	1.04	9.0	.92
4.0	1.02	10.0	.90
5.0	1.00 (standard)		

By such a formula the operator can enhance his incentive earnings on production by as much as 10 percent by paying strict attention to quality; conversely, he can be penalized up to 10 percent of incentive earnings by inattention to quality.

Obviously, exact values and the extent of the quantity multiplier will depend on the cost and quality factors in the particular case. Yield factors (the ratio of usable product from given quantities of input material) will also vary.

Incentives for Indirect Operations

A relatively recent application of incentives is to indirect operations. The development is sound and necessary, and such incentives must receive serious managerial attention if industry is to maintain required levels of productivity. Many attempts to develop incentives for indirect work have followed the techniques used in measuring direct work, and those techniques (stopwatch studies and standard data development) have been relatively successful in some applications such as maintenance. However, a complete approach to measurement of indirect labor requires many different techniques. For example, considerable progress is being made with the use of the computer-developed multivariant formulas described in Chapter 13.

The application of standards and incentives to building maintenance generally requires detailed planning of assignments and the calculation of standard times for the work to be done. Major savings in indirect labor have thereby been accomplished, but, in general, the administrative costs preclude the application of this type of control to any but the largest organizations.

Accounting practice tends to categorize direct labor as the elements of work that are directly concerned with the production of parts or assemblies. Indirect labor is then considered as any activity that cannot be directly allocated to such production but does serve to support the manufacturing effort by supplying general services. Such services must be then included with the product cost on some empirical basis. However, the distinctions are meaningless from the standpoint of measurement for incentive purposes.

Some work classed as indirect may be highly repetitive, such as drill sharpening, cutter grinding, or some types of shipping operations. The procedures may be well standardized, and conventional time study, standard data application, and use of direct incentives (standard-hour or a similar plan) is frequently very satisfactory.

As with normal, direct work, the indirect functions in every plant will vary from well-structured operations such as those just described to work that is not directly measurable by conventional methods. Thus, it is the characteristic feature of the work being done that determines the most suitable type of measurement and ultimate incentive treatment rather than classification as direct or indirect.

The application of incentives to indirect labor should follow the same basic principles as those that apply to direct work. The best match of specific plans to the various types of work being done is offered in Chapter 5. The matching of plans and work applies to indirect work just as much as it does to direct work.

There are, however, a few cases of indirect work that are not susceptible to measurement of output, or where control of output is external. For example, a crane operator in an erection shop must be available at all times, but he may be idle for long periods of time. His function is to service others, and his activities are determined largely by requests for service from the erection floor. Regardless of motivation, he cannot perform any more lifts than are called for. Similarly, a guard at the plant gate cannot do any more than follow routines for admittance and promptly report emergencies or unusual situations. These are two situations in which the introduction of any type of incentive is impractical and merely becomes a gift, but such situations are uncommon. The other areas of indirect work are usually well suited to some type of incentive under the general principles outlined in Chapter 5.

Careful planning and study of indirect work will yield attractive savings. Since indirect work is characteristically not as well planned or organized as repetitive production operations, the potential for improvement through better organization of work, methods study, and ultimate use of incentives is often greater than when the same industrial engineering effort is applied to direct labor.

Supervisory Incentives

The success or failure of any incentive plan is so closely tied in with the administration of the plan by shop supervision that there are many arguments in favor of developing a supervisory incentive or bonus based on the performance of the incentive plan. However, such a plan must recognize all of the functions for which a supervisor should be held responsible.

A supervisory plan that relates a bonus to such factors as incentive gains or incentive coverage inevitably places the foreman in the same position as the employee in desiring the most liberal incentives. It completely neglects his overall function, which is to produce a quality product at lowest possible cost and in compliance with production schedules. Neglect of that principle has sometimes led to open warfare between foremen and industrial engineers or their counterparts. It may also lead to abuse of the incentive plan by foremen in permitting extra daywork or allowances in conjunction with unpopular rates or by failure to comply with delivery schedules because of certain rate dissatisfactions.

Bonuses for the foremen should encourage cooperation in improving methods and reducing direct labor costs as well as overhead labor expenses. Additional factors should be weighted to include quality and schedule compliance. The bonus should not be based on the performance of the individual department alone. At least one-third and preferably one-half of the potential bonus should be based on overall plant or division performance by the same general yardsticks as used for the individual department. The purpose here is to prevent

Table 1. Factors for use with supervisory bonus.

Factor	Usual Method of Measurement	Suggested Weighting in Formula
Direct labor performance	$\dfrac{\text{Standard hours produced}}{\text{Actual hours}}$	Light
Incentive coverage	$\dfrac{\text{Hours on standard}}{\text{Total direct hours}}$	Light
Excess ratio*	$\dfrac{\text{Total hours factory excess accounts}}{\text{Total standard hours}}$	Medium
Support ratio†	$\dfrac{\text{Total hours factory support accounts}}{\text{Total standard hours}}$	Medium
Overhead ratio	$\dfrac{\text{Standard variable budget}}{\text{Actual overhead}}$	Medium
Material usage	$\dfrac{\text{Standard material usage}}{\text{Actual material usage}}$	Heavy
Factory supplies	$\dfrac{\text{Standard or budget}}{\text{Actual}}$	Medium to heavy
Schedule compliance	Percent schedule completed on time	Heavy
Unit cost reduction	Requires individual development	Heavy

* Excess accounts include such items as rework, lost time, waiting for materials, machine breakdown, and repair to product.

† Support accounts include such items as material handling, tool maintenance, inspection, setups, and machine and equipment maintenance.

Note: Top performance in all areas should result in bonus payments of 25 to 30 percent of base salary.

the individual foreman from attempting to make a good showing for his department at the expense of other departments in the plant. The development of this type of incentive seldom follows fixed patterns. The installation must be designed to suit the particular application involved.

Table 1 outlines the various factors that could be used in developing a supervisory bonus in accordance with the principles outlined here. The table shows usual methods of measuring the factors together with suggested weightings. The actual weightings to be used will, of course, depend on the relative importance of the various factors to the successful operation of the firm.

3

The Measurement Factor

A NUMBER OF factors other than advantages, disadvantages, and mathematical treatment affect wage incentive plans. Foremost among them are leveling, individual plans versus group plans, predetermined time systems, machine- or process-controlled operations, development of standard data, and training allowances. A study of these factors is a prerequisite to a discussion of the applicability of various types of incentive plans to specific industrial situations.

Leveling

The discussions of relative earnings at varying performance levels in Chapter 2 assumed some understanding of the techniques of performance rating. For the benefit of the nontechnical reader, performance rating, or leveling, as it is frequently called, is one of the most controversial areas of the entire work measurement field. Leveling is the process by which the time study man adjusts the observed times of the operator being studied to some concept of the pace of the "average worker." That is, his purpose is to adjust the times developed by a slow worker and those developed by a fast worker to some accepted standard of average performance.

We have here the dual function of defining a standard of performance in recognizable terms and evaluating observed performance

35

by that standard. Unfortunately, even the best-written descriptions of performance levels are difficult to relate to specific performances on shop work, since they are completely objective in their approach. The two generally accepted versions of performance, or pace, are "*normal pace*" and "*incentive pace.*"

NORMAL PACE

The normal pace is also known as *daywork normal* or *normal task*. It is considered to be the pace of an average well-trained and capable operator who is familiar with the work being done but is working under non-incentive conditions. It is this work pace that is used as normal in most of the training films on leveling, such as those distributed by the Society for the Advancement of Management. The construction of many incentive plans makes this pace the point at which incentive earnings begin.

INCENTIVE PACE

The incentive pace is also known as *high task*. It refers to a rate of output that can reasonably be maintained day after day by the experienced operator who is well trained in the type of work he is doing and who is motivated by a suitable incentive. The definition also presumes a level of performance equivalent to that required to attain median incentive earnings.

Attempts at quantitative definitions of pace are largely lacking, but much good work has been done with training films such as those developed by the Society for the Advancement of Management and others. Normal pace has also been defined as the pace involved in dealing 52 cards in .50 minute, walking on a level surface at 3 miles per hour, or filling a standard pin board with 30 pins in .41 minute by using a two-handed method. However, it is difficult to relate such definitions to shop operations, and much reliance must be placed on the judgment of the time study man.

The various rating films probably make their greatest contribution in training time study men and in serving general educational purposes. Unfortunately, there is no proven correlation between the ability of a time study man to level motion pictures and his ability to maintain identical levels of value, judgment, and consistency in rating specific operations in the industrial plant. In addition, there is no universal concept of normal performance throughout industry. The level of performance of a well-trained operator of a power sewing machine who is working on highly repetitive operations cannot be compared directly with levels of performance in machine tool building, for example. There simply is no common denominator of such a variety of work situations.

The dealing of 52 playing cards in .50 minute or walking at a speed of 3 miles per hour has been considered as normal performance by averaging opinions of a large number of experienced time study men, but neither performance permits a meaningful translation to such work as operating a punch press or a machine tool, welding, or doing repetitive hand assembly, nor does either permit evaluation of skill factors. The popular definition of a fair day's work is verbal only and is translatable into numerical values only in the skilled judgment of a trained observer. Unfortunately, up to the present, we have not developed any better means of measuring performance. Those who are interested in exploring this subject more thoroughly will find excellent material in Niebel[1] and Barnes.[2]

The mathematical procedures for adjusting incentive payment plans to the concept of normal pace or incentive pace are seldom clearly understood by the layman—or by industrial engineering students at the graduate level, for that matter. Therefore, it is not surprising that there are numerous misconceptions in management circles.

In the preceding paragraphs, normal pace and incentive pace are defined in generally objective terms and a few examples of normal pace (walking, dealing cards, inserting pins) have been given. There is a good area of agreement among industrial engineers that the general ratio of performance (pieces per hour, or any similar measure) between normal pace and incentive pace is approximately in the ratio of 125 percent (if normal pace = 100, then incentive pace = 125) for the average individual. There is also general agreement that the corresponding incentive gain should not be less than the 25 percent.

If we so design our incentive plan that incentive earnings begin at our accepted concept of normal pace, then the mathematics of the specific plan will determine the earnings when incentive pace is reached. The alternative procedures are illustrated in the following example, which is based on dealing a deck of 52 cards in .50 minute as an accepted level of normal pace.

[1] Benjamin W. Niebel, *Motion and Time Study* 4th Ed. (Homewood, Ill.: Richard D. Irwin, Inc., 1967), Chap. 15.
[2] Ralph M. Barnes, *Motion and Time Study: Design and Measurement of Work,* 6th Ed. (New York: John Wiley & Sons, Inc., 1968), Chap. 22.

EXAMPLE. The calculation is based first on normal pace and then on incentive pace.

Normal pace	100%
Observed cycle time	.50 minute
Leveled at 100%	.50 minute

$$\text{Production per hour} = \frac{60 \text{ minutes}}{.50 \text{ minute}} \quad 120 \text{ pieces per hour}$$

$$\text{Standard} = \frac{1.0 \text{ hour}}{120 \text{ pieces}} \times 100 \quad .83 \text{ hour per 100 pieces}$$

Incentive pace	100%
Observed cycle time min	.50 minute
Leveled at 80% (100 ÷ 125)	.40 minute
Incentive allowance of 25%	.10 minute
Time allowed = .40 + .10	.50 minute
Standard	.83 hour per 100 pieces (as above)

We note that 52 cards in .50 minute is equivalent to 120 decks per hour. Neglecting fatigue or delay allowances, for simplicity, the standard would then probably be expressed as .83 hour per 100 decks (1 hour divided by 120 decks). The usual concept of incentive pace (25 percent improvement over normal performance) should then result in a production of 150 decks per hour (125 percent of the standard of 120 decks per hour), and the operator would then earn 1.25 hours (150 decks times .83 hour per 100) for each hour and would therefore achieve incentive gains of 25 percent.

The procedure described presumes that time studies are leveled to the concept of normal pace as 100 percent. The same standard of .83 hour per 100 pieces can also be arrived at when leveling to incentive pace as 100 percent, as shown in the second calculation.

What we are saying in the second calculation is that when the operator is at incentive pace, we expect his time per piece to be reduced to .40 minute. Since we expect to pay 125 percent incentive gain at this level of performance, we add the incentive allowance of 25 percent to develop the standard time.

Although the two procedures illustrated in the example can produce identical standards, the concept of leveling to normal pace causes difficulties in operations in which there are substantial proportions of machine- or process-controlled times. Since those times are beyond the control of the operator, there is no potential for improvement in them and it is impossible for the operator to achieve expected incentive gains for those elements. As a result, the use of a special adjustment, usually called machine or process allowance, is required to permit median incentive gains for the elements of work that are controlled. Because of that requirement, systems that relate incentive pace to desired median incentive gains, as in the second calculation of the preceding example, are preferable. There are three arguments for that system:

1. Median earnings at incentive pace are the usual benchmarks at union-management incentive discussions.

2. When an incentive plan is in existence, incentive pace is more in evidence and can be observed, and time study comparisons between incentive operations then become more meaningful.

3. The mathematics of the method of leveling to incentive pace eliminates the need for separate adjustments for machine- or process-controlled elements.

Group Versus Individual Plans

Any of the direct measurement plans described in Chapter 2 can be applied on either a group basis or an individual basis. The decision should be based on the general characteristics of the work being performed.

In an individual plan, each employee's compensation is based on his own effort. The general result is higher production rates and lower unit costs. Individual plans are particularly suitable when the production runs are fairly long and consist of repetitive, measurable work and when there is little need for the cooperative efforts of other individuals. Because of their strong incentive appeal, individual plans are generally preferable to group plans provided the nature of the work permits the choice.

Group plans are ordinarily used when two or more persons are working as a team on assignments or when output depends on co-operation between individuals in the group. An example would be two or more individuals loading or unloading a railroad car or an assembly line on which the operations are progressive from one end of the line to the other and output can be increased by good coopera-tion between individuals. Another example would be a shipping room in which not only is there an interdependence of the efforts of indi-viduals but also the problem of assigning specific credits for work done by each individual becomes impractical from a timekeeping standpoint. Group plans have the advantages of easy installation be-cause much organization of the work can be done by the group and the administrative costs (timekeeping) are generally much lower.

Since group plans inevitably represent an averaging of the performance levels of all the individuals in the group, incentive gains do
not show the fluctuation observed in individual plans.

The individual incentive is generally favored by most industrial
engineers whenever its application is practical, largely for the reason
that the incentive appeal is somewhat stronger. For example, a survey
of wage incentive practices among southeastern Wisconsin firms, conducted by the Milwaukee Chapter of the Society for the Advancement
of Management, shows that in 25 companies using individual incentives the average gain was 140 percent above base rate, whereas
the corresponding gain for 14 companies using group incentives was
136 percent over base rate. Group plans, particularly those that are
plantwide, are a social device, and they appeal to many who have
a strong industrial relations philosophy. They stress the self-policing
aspects of group organization as well as decreased administrative
costs. Obviously, the philosophy of the top level of management will
have a very considerable bearing on the choice of plans.

Predetermined Times

The use of predetermined times as a substitute for conventional
stopwatch techniques is increasing rapidly. These times are derived
from intensive research work, much of it done with high-speed mo-
tion-picture cameras. They represent times that are normal and are
therefore not subject to the vagaries of the leveling procedure. By
the use of predetermined times it is possible to develop a time standard for any type of manual operation once the motion pattern has
been determined. The times so developed are consistent and, assuming
that the motion patterns have been correctly interpreted, highly
reliable.

Predetermined times are based on tabulated values for all con-
ceivable types or combinations of body member movements: reach,
grasp, transport, transfer, and position, all with modifications for dis-
tance traveled and weight moved. Predetermined times can readily
be used to develop tables of standard data for application to similar
work patterns. But although they do not require skill in leveling, there
are definite areas in which trained judgment is required by the observer in order to properly identify complex motion patterns.

Predetermined time systems are not new; the original concept,
motion-time analysis, was developed by A. B. Segur in 1924. Among
others are the Work Factor System, by J. H. Quick, W. J. Shea, and

R. E. Koehler, and Methods-Time Measurement (MTM) by H. B. Maynard, G. J. Stegemerten, and J. I. Schwab. The MTM system is one of the most widely recognized systems in use today.

A more recent development in this area is UnivEl, which was developed in 1964 by Management Science, Inc., Appleton, Wisconsin. UnivEl is a computer-oriented system. It does not require the detailed analysis of each micromotion, the writing out of the method description, or reference to chart values, since all those functions are coded for computer printouts. The system shows considerable promise and is being installed in a growing number of industries. It will be discussed more fully in Chapter 13.

All of the predetermined time systems require the development of the optimum method by conventional motion study and work simplification techniques; and since time is determined by method, it is equally important that the standard method be followed exactly. That, of course, is true of any system of work measurement.

There are two limitations to most predetermined time systems. The first of these is that it is extremely difficult to evaluate simultaneous motions, that is, simultaneous motions of the right and left hand or motions that are controlled by process limitations such as sanding, brushing, and painting. In addition, process- or machine-controlled elements of an operation must still be determined by conventional methods, since the predetermined times are limited to manual motions alone.

Machine- or Process-Controlled Operations

Any incentive plan involving operations in which there is a considerable element of machine- or process-controlled time requires careful study of potential incentive opportunities. That is particularly true if the method of leveling is to normal task. When a substantial percentage of elements are fixed by being machine- or process-controlled, there is little that the operator can do to change those time values, and unless compensating adjustments are made, the potential incentive opportunity is reduced accordingly.

In the past, there was some reasoning that, since the operator was not exerting incentive effort during machine- or process-controlled operations, he was not entitled to normal incentive gains for that time. That conclusion was based on the principle that extra earnings result from extra effort. However, strict application of the principle led to considerable disparity of incentive gains between employees on manual operations and those on machine-controlled operations. That in turn led to difficulties in transferring employees from one type of work to the other. Union complaints concerning unequal incentive opportunity became frequent.

The trend today is to consider the man and machine as a complete unit and to adjust the standards for the machine-controlled elements to produce expected incentive gains for optimum operation of the unit. The practice of allowing normal incentive gains on machine-paced operations or elements of such operations is more consistent with that attitude. The mathematics of the incentive is then constructed to develop optimum output at lowest total unit cost. This subject will be discussed more in detail in Chapter 4.

Standard Data

One of the important criteria in evaluating the effectiveness of a standards department is the extent to which the department has been able to develop adequate and reliable standard data. All time studies should be designed with a thought of ultimate conversion of the time values to tables, formulas, or curves—that is the ultimate goal of the work measurement function. The principle of standard data application is not new; in fact, it was proposed by Frederick W. Taylor in his early investigations on the art of cutting metals. He envisioned the development of standard times for various kinds of work that could be universally used in industry. Although the development has not been precisely as he intended, it has proceeded, and along two different lines.

Predetermined standard times developed by methods-time measurement (MTM), master standard data (MSD), and work factor are essentially standard data. Their use requires a high degree of standardization of work in the most minute detail, together with proper recording and training of the operator in the precise method to be used. When operations fall into general classifications, various common elements of work can, of course, be totaled into larger units to avoid the extremely detailed analysis and addition of hundreds of minute elements. The accuracy of this approach to standard data development is limited by the adherence of the actual operation to the planned methods. Since all the values used in the tabulations are based on leveled performance, all the variables introduced by operator performance ratings are averaged out.

Standard data developed from time studies can be equally effective and reliable and in many cases can be developed through much simpler procedures. A key measure to the success of the method lies in the proper selection of elements and absolute uniformity in the use of break points. Without such preplanned organization of time study techniques, standard data developed from time study will be inconsistent and mathematically invalid. That is the underlying reason for the difficulty in attempting to develop standard data from collections of old time studies, frequently those made by different individuals. Overlapping of elements, varying descriptions, and inconsistencies in selecting break points render most old time studies useless for developing standard data. Unfortunately, much of the available textbook material on standard data development is still confined to the micrometric approach. That approach requires that the technician applying the standard must select the method for the particular operation, list the proper sequence of handling elements, and pick off values from tables of data. For example:

1. Place part on jig, place drill bushing.
2. Move to position.
3. Bring drill to work.
4. Drill one hole (speed-feed formula).
5. Raise drill.
6. Move to reamer.
7. Remove drill bushing.
8. Bring reamer to work.
9. Ream (speed-feed formula).
10. Raise reamer.
11. Remove part from jig.

Values must be determined for these various elements by referring to tables based on the weight of the part and complexity of the fixture. Machining times are probably determined from formulas. After all of the times are selected from tables of standard data, they are totaled, standard allowances are inserted, and the time is converted to a standard.[3] Although standard data so applied have all of the advantages of consistency and have minimized much repetitive time study, the entire process of standards application becomes somewhat laborious. The reason is that the logic or methods development

---

[3] Much valuable material typical of this approach is included in Ralph Barnes, *Motion and Time Study: Design and Measurement of Work*, 6th Ed., (New York: John Wiley & Sons, Inc., 1968).

of standard data from such sources for a part such as a gear blank to be turned, faced, drilled, and reamed in a turret lathe could conceivably require a full sheet of calculations listing all manual elements as well as computed machine times for the various cuts. See Table 2 for a typical example.

In such a situation if we were to assume that the given plant

Table 2. Gear blanks—turn, face rim, drill, and ream in Warner & Swasey turret lathe.

Elements	Manual Time, Minutes	Machine Time, Minutes
1. Pick up casing from pallet, chuck in four-jaw chuck	1.00	
2. Start machine	.02	
3. Advance hexagonal turret to work	.07	
4. Turn OD (10 inches diam., 1½ inches wide), 40 rpm, .012 inch per rev. feed		3.20
5. Advance side turret to work, engage feed	(.05)*	
6. Face rim (10 inches diam., 1 inch thick) (40 rpm, .012 inch per rev. feed)		(1.70)*
7. Disengage feed, back off side turret	(.07)*	
8. Position hexagonal turret to clear, index, advance to work	.06	
9. Change spindle speed	.10	
10. Center drill (hand feed, ½ inch deep)		.20
11. Position hexagonal turret to clear, index, advance to work	.06	
12. Drill, 1 inch diam. by 2 inches long		.55
13. Position hexagonal turret to clear, index, and advance to work	.06	
14. Change spindle speed	.10	
15. Ream drilled holes, hand feed		.20
16. Break edge on rim, hand file		.15
17. Stop spindle	.04	
18. Remove from four-jaw chuck and set aside	.40	
Base time per piece	1.91	4.30

* These operations are done while the outer diameter is turned (operation 4). They are considered internal and so are not included in totals.

Note: Delay, fatigue, and other allowances are neglected for simplicity.

manufactured a variety of gear blanks ranging from, let us say, 5 to 15 inches in diameter, studies might reveal that the predominant independent variables would be diameter and width of gear face. Thus, a few selected applications of the micrometric data throughout the size range could develop a family of curves as shown in Figure 2, and then the appropriate standard time for a given diameter and width could be selected from the curves. This type of standard data reduces clerical effort to a minimum and still retains all of the advantages of consistent data together with almost instantaneous application of the standard. The macrometric or objective approach to standard data has wide application to most manufacturing situations.

At the present time, most process engineering is parts-oriented. A study of the actual manufacturing methods, however, will show

Figure 2. Standard time for turning outer diameter, facing rim, and drilling and reaming cast-iron gears on a Warner & Swasey turret lathe.

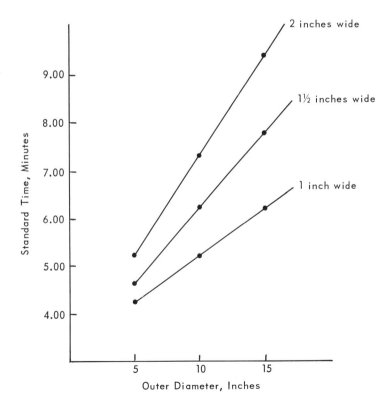

that much work is done on highly similar parts such as shafts, gears, and bearings and the major independent variable is confined to simple factors such as length, diameter, and weight. Thus, the objective approach calls for the development of tables or curves for family groups. If that has been accomplished, a uniformly consistent standard can be applied almost instantaneously from a single chart of data by using the predominant variable for the particular part in question. The ability of a standards department to develop objective standard data is important to the effectiveness of the industrial engineering effort. For a more detailed discussion of this approach to standard data, reference is made to the very excellent presentation in *How to Chart Standard Data*, by Phil Carroll.[4]

Another type of standard data is a list of all possible combinations of work elements that could be performed on a single machine tool together with elemental times. The analyst merely has to circle the specific elements and add up the time analysis to develop the rate. A typical example of this approach is Figure 3.

Training Allowances

For many years, various types of training allowances have been paid in industry, and, in support of them, recent developments in the use of progress curves indicate that most industrial work is indeed subject to continuing improvement. For example, records of productivity in airframe assembly and machine tool erection indicate consistent improvement each time the volume of work done is doubled; in assembly work, improvement in performance is approximately 80 percent each time the volume of work is doubled. Furthermore, research indicates that this kind of improvement continues over large quantities of work and considerable lapses of time. An example is the change in erection time of a new model of a machine tool, Figure 4. The slope of the curve graphically illustrates the hazard of applying permanent incentive rates in the early stages of a complicated operation.[5]

Another difficulty arises when training requires a considerable period of time and the existing standards are based on the performance of a trained operator. One successful approach to this problem involved an operation that consisted of applying conducting silver

[4] New York: McGraw-Hill, 1960.
[5] See Raymond Jordan, *How to Use The Learning Curve* (Boston: Materials Management Institute, 1966) for a thorough discussion of the application of progress curves to industrial work.

Figure 3. Worksheet for job-estimating drill press operations.
(Reproduced by courtesy of E. A. Cyrol & Company, Chicago, Illinois.)

Job:		Part:						
Operation:				Oper. No.:				
Date:	Set Up Hrs.:			Std. Hrs. Per 100				

Element	Hi Spd.	Light Duty	Med. Duty	Hvy. Duty	Occ	Minutes
1. Load & Unload	.07	.10	.18	.27		
2. Lock & Unlock: Toggle or Cam Lever Per Ea.	.02	.02	.03	.04		
Lock scr. or Star Whl. Per Ea.	.06	.06	.09	.09		
Allen scr. or Hex. Nut Per Ea.	.13	.13	.14	.15		
ADD'L. if necessary to: rem. & plc. scr. or nut	.07	.07	.08	.09		
pos. strap clamp or hinge cover	.03	.04	.05	.05		
(Per Each) rem. & plc. strap clamp	.08	.08	.10	.10		
rem. & plc. template or cover	.11	.14	.17	.21		
3. Blow off table, jib, etc. Per Surface	.03	.04	.05	.06		
4. Pos. jig to spindle: No stops or rails Per Spindle	.03	.04	.06	.08		
Stops a/o rails Per Spindle	.03	.03	.04	.04		
5. Hole to Hole: 0-5" Distance Per Hole	.02	.03	.04	.05		
Over 5" Distance Per Hole	.03	.05	.06	.07		
6. Lower & Raise spindle: No locating Per Occ	.03	.03	.04	.05		
Locate hole Per Occ	.04	.04	.05	.07		
7. Plc. & remove bushing Per Occ	.05	.05	.08	.08		
8. Tumble jig (or part) Per Occ	.02	.03	.04	.05		
9. Brush lubricant .03 X _____ Tools = _____ ÷ _____ Pcs.						
10. Gauging .08 X _____ Dims. = _____ ÷ _____ Pcs.						
11. Change Tools: Quick Change Chuck .10 Per Occ						
Keyed Drill Chuck .25 Per Occ						

Machining Elements	Depth of Cut *	SFM	RPM	Feed	Inches Per Min.	
Spot Drill or Chf.: 0-1/2" .03, Over 1/2" .05						

Tool Care:	Total Mach. Time _____ X 8%	
*Incl. Drill Point Set Up Hours .20 Hrs.	a. Total Minutes	
Plus .06 Hrs. X _____ Tools = _____ Hrs.	b. Plus % Allowances	
Total Set Up _____ Hrs.	c. Total Production Minutes	
	d. Std. Hrs. Per 100	

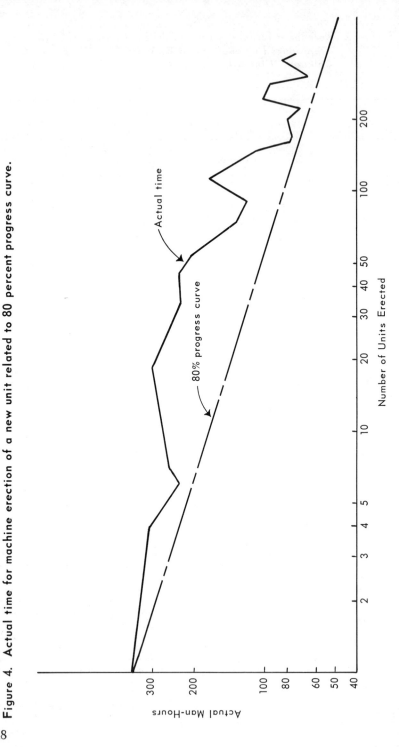

Figure 4. Actual time for machine erection of a new unit related to 80 percent progress curve.

paint to both sides of thin ceramic discs ranging in size from 1/4 inch to about 3/4 inch. The operation involved a complicated series of manual elements with nonrhythmic motion patterns, beginning with loading the disks on a multiple holder from a vibratory feeder, placing this holder under a silk-screening device for painting the first side, subsequent drying, inverting into a second holding fixture, and then silk screening the second side with subsequent drying and unloading onto a firing screen. The complicated sequence of elements, as well as stringent quality requirements, required a lengthy learning process. Natural rhythm was difficult to acquire because of the nature of the operation.

Numerous time studies confirmed the existing incentives and allowances and indicated that the experienced operators were making satisfactory incentive gains. However, the studies did show that the complicated requirements of the job confused the newer operators so that they failed to learn the intricate motion patterns. Because of significant increases in production schedules, quite a number of new people were hired, but they either quit after three to six weeks on the job or requested transfer to other work. In addition, some of the older, more experienced operators were leaving for normal reasons; exit interviews, established that they were not dissatisfied with the work.

Numerous avenues were explored to find a solution to the personnel problem. Interviews with new operators indicated that the only common denominator seemed to be a general discouragement and a feeling that the newer operators could never attain the output of the more experienced girls. Initial experiments with learning time allowances did not produce any significant improvement.

To develop more significant data on the learning characteristics of the job, the average performance of new operators versus the number of weeks on the job was plotted on logarithmic coordinates, Figure 5. The curves predicted 26 weeks of training for the average new operator to reach the expected level of incentive gain for experienced operators. Incidentally, the curve on logarithmic scale very closely approximated the 85 percent improvement curve quite common in similar work in other industries.

The course decided on was to develop a training allowance over the 26-week period that would enable an operator learning at an average rate to begin with daywork earnings of approximately 10 percent above daywork for the first week and then gradually increase those earnings to expected incentive gains at the end of the 26-week training period. The solution is indicated graphically in Figure 6, which shows the average performance of new operators taken from Figure 5, but plotted on rectangular coordinates.

Also shown is the relative performance expected to result from application of training allowance over the 26-week period. Note that this curve begins at 118 percent for the first week and ends at 160 percent at the end of the 26-week period. The figures shown at the top of the graph give the percent, which is added to the average performance for each week of the training period in order to obtain the expected relative performance. These percentages start at 68 percent for the first week and gradually decrease to 5 percent at the end of the 26th week, when they stop. Standard rates for work done were increased by those percents to augment the learner's incentive earnings, and the excess over the standard rate was charged to a training account.

The incentive plan in use was the Halsey 50-50 plan. Standards were expressed in hours per 100 units of production. Thus, if an operator earned 12 standard hours in an 8-hour day, the 4 hours saved would be split 50-50 and 2 hours would be credited to the operator, which would give her a standard-hour earning of 10 hours in an 8-hour day, or 125 percent. Thus the curves in Figure 6 indicate relative performance in total standard hours earned, and a relative performance of 160 percent represents 130 percent incentive gain payable to the operator.

The plan was introduced to the operators by a careful explanation

Figure 5. Average performance of new operators on a multiple-screening job. *(Plotted on a logarithmic scale.)*

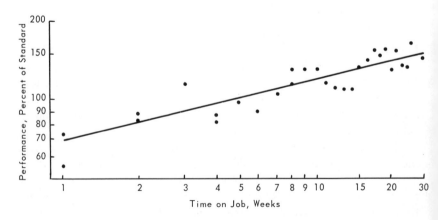

Time on Job, Weeks

Figure 6.   Development of training allowance for multiple-screening operation.

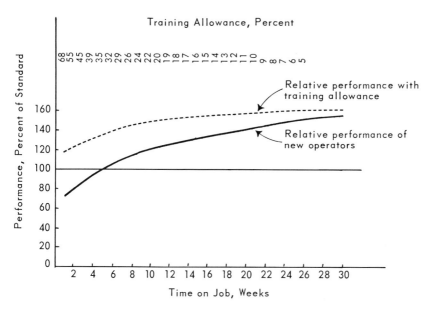

covering all steps in the process. Particularly emphasized was the incentive: If the trainees were as effective as the average operator under learning conditions, they could expect to earn a 9 percent incentive during the first week and have a gradual increase to a 30 percent incentive gain by the twenty-sixth week. They were also told that the twenty-sixth week would conclude the learning allowance. A detailed analysis of the proper work method was prepared, and a copy was given to each trainee. Only qualified operators were used for instruction, and the foremen observed the training closely and frequently checked progress.

Six months after the plan went into effect, most of the employees who were present at the initiation of the program, and most of those hired after it, had remained on the job. Losses in employment can now be attributed to normal turnover. Morale has risen. Employees from other departments frequently request transfers into the area. Earnings have been better than expected, with usual incentive benefits to both the company and the employees.

One interesting point to note is that the 26-week training period has been shortened; that is, the rate of learning has increased and thus reduced the learning time. It is felt that the improvement in learning time is due in a considerable measure to the use of the training allowance. Before the inception of the allowance, new operators were paid the guaranteed hourly rate when their production was below standard. Thus, during the learning period, they received no more than day rate for as much as 5 weeks for the average operator, in spite of some improvement in performance during that time. That so discouraged most of the new operators that they either quit or requested transfer. With the training allowances, there has been a gradual increase in their weekly earnings from the beginning, and they can relate those increased earnings to increased proficiency on the job. The net result to the company has also been favorable: The cost of the learning allowance was considerably less than the prior cost of adjusting earnings to day rate under conditions of unsatisfactory earnings and high turnover rates.

In summary, the study of past performance by new operators provided a means of establishing a training period of known reliability. Various industries have used allowances in different ways to supplement incentive earnings during the training period. In this particular situation it was decided to use a multiplying factor to increase the standard rates; in other situations the same result has been attained by the addition of daywork time in gradually decreasing amounts until the supplement disappears at the end of the stipulated training period. Usually these more empirical procedures create frictions that tend to thwart the positive features found here.

Supplementing incentive earnings under a training program such as that described performs several valuable functions. It recognizes the effect of the learning curve on performance and eliminates much of the negative pressure on the incentive system. Unsatisfactory incentive gains by inexperienced operators are no longer an adverse morale factor.

The principle of supplementing learner incentive performance becomes useful whenever the introduction of a new or inexperienced operator into a group represents potential impairment of the incentive earnings of the group. The group can be charged only with the portion of the learner's time represented by his expected progress on a learning curve. The difference between the time of the learner charged into the group and his full working day can be supplemented to the learner on a daywork basis and charged to the learning account. Thus, if the learning curve indicates that at some point in time the learner is 50 percent effective, the group is charged for 4 hours of his time for an 8-hour day. The learner receives 4 hours of incentive pay at the group's normal earning rate plus 4 hours of daywork charged to the learning account.

The procedure has worked well in numerous types of groups, including shipping room and conveyorized assembly lines. It avoids penalizing the older members of the group for the inefficiency of the newcomer and encourages them to train the learner in the most rapid possible way.

4

Kinds of Industrial Operations

WHICH INCENTIVE PLAN is best suited to a given situation depends on the proper evaluation of a number of interrelated and frequently conflicting factors. To begin with, the plan must be suitable to the type of work being performed. There are numerous general kinds of work in industry, and they range from standard repetitive operations to work that is not readily measurable by conventional means. In addition, basic management philosophies, union-management relations, and the capabilities of the industrial engineering function may modify the selection. This chapter will discuss the general types of work and also some of the less tangible factors that affect selection of a plan or plans.

For our purposes we will use the following categories of work: standardized repetitive operations with either low obsolescence or frequent technological or design change, semistandardized operations, unstandardized operations, process-controlled operations, and work not directly measurable.

Standardized Repetitive Operations

OPERATIONS WITH LOW OBSOLESCENCE

In general, methods for the manual work done in this category are well established and standardized. Frequently there is a high manual content in the various assembly operations and also considerable individual or personal control of performance. The production volume justifies a high level of development in tooling and special equipment and considerable mechanization of parts manufacturing. Materials and working conditions are usually quite uniform. Such work is readily measurable by conventional means and is frequently well suited to measurement by some of the predetermined time systems. The substantial amount of direct labor justifies a high degree of sophistication in any industrial engineering effort. That effort should include careful application of the principles of motion economy, operation analysis, standardized procedures, and detailed written instructions. There is good justification for meticulous work measurement techniques and also extensive use of predetermined times. For example, if the production on a certain part is 10 million pieces per year and the hourly labor cost is $2.50 per hour including fringes, a time savings of .01 minute on an operation is equivalent to an annual savings in direct labor of approximately $4000 per year.

OPERATIONS WITH FREQUENT CHANGES

Examples of standardized repetitive operations with frequent changes for reason of technology or design are assembly of small power tools and appliances, and radio and television parts and chassis. The characteristics of this type of work are quite similar to those of the preceding type, except that generally there will be a higher manual content in the operations and less special tooling or fixturing; a greater proportion of the work will be done with general-purpose tooling or equipment. Methods, however, are usually well established and standardized, so that measurement techniques will be similar to those applicable to operations with low obsolescence. Conventional time study procedures are usually applied, and there is good justification for the use of predetermined times. Because of the frequent technological changes and obsolescence expected, written standard practice instructions become highly important as a record of how specific operations were performed. The frequency of product-process change will accentuate problems relating to operator training, and learning curves will assume greater importance. There will be more temporary manual operations while mechanized methods are being developed.

In this type of work the development of standard data assumes considerable importance. Standard data, with their consistency, uniformity, and economy of application, become of extreme value when a great many standards are to be applied.

Semistandardized Operations

Examples of products of this category are large appliances and medium-cost mechanical items of all types. Such operations are also typical of small manufacturing companies that supply components to larger users. In this type of work, orders are usually released in varying quantities and runs are of moderately short duration. As a result, manufacturing methods are based largely on general-purpose tooling and equipment and less attention is paid to the refinement of assembly operations. There is often substantial variation in materials, tooling, and methods.

Written standard practice sheets or operation analyses become of great importance in order to preserve a history of the method for use in subsequent production runs. Time study usually follows conventional stopwatch methods, and there is less reliance on predetermined time systems. The development of good consistent standard data assumes primary importance, since the work is characterized by large groupings of parts being made in small quantities. The arrangement and techniques of time study practice should all be directed toward ultimately developing the greatest amount of standard data.

Unstandardized Operations

Typical of this work would be job shops making a few units of special items to customer order, tool and die making, repair work, and special machine tools. The planning of the work and methods must in most cases be done by the operator. It is difficult to justify anything except the most elementary type of methods analysis unless there is strong probability of repeat orders. Operations of this nature generally require basic skills and abilities on the part of the operator to devise his own methods, and there is little need for training in the usual sense of the word. Tooling is generally elementary and limited to holding devices or jigs to locate drilled holes.

Instead of conventional time study, reliance must be placed on estimates, past records, and the simpler means of measurement.

Process-controlled Operations

Here the rate of output is largely controlled by the process or by mechanical equipment; examples are leather tanning, brewing, plastic molding, automatic screw machines, and some of the newer types of tape-controlled machining centers. Proper control of the method or process frequently is more important than maximum labor efficiency. In many cases, attempts to increase production by changing machine speeds or process times may result in faulty work or damage. The operator's function is mainly that of supplying material, removing finished parts, and generally supervising performance of the machine or the process.

Generally, little measurement is involved in this type of operation beyond recording proper machine speeds or process conditions at the point where optimum output and quality are obtained. Conventional time study procedures are frequently inapplicable except as a means of recording delay times and the incidence of noncyclic elements. Performance measurement can frequently be directly related to output or production records.

Work Not Directly Measurable

Examples here would be machine repairing, maintenance work, experimentation, model making, and mechanical development. Not only is such work not measurable by the ordinary techniques relating to time input, but proper credit for the amount of work done is frequently difficult to ascertain. The work typifies the saying that as the degree of mental or planning functions increases, the stopwatch becomes virtually useless. In the past, very little work of this type has been successfully placed on incentives, although some use has been made of cost ratio plans or other systems of indirect incentives. Occasionally, standards of output may be developed through multiple regression analyses.

The six categories of work done in the industrial plant have been described largely from the standpoint of their relation to work measurement procedures. Practically every company will have a mixture of the various kinds, including those industries that produce a standardized product in large quantities. Even in those industries there will be many areas in which work is process-controlled, or where short runs prevail, or where some of the work is unmeasurable by conventional techniques.

The type of incentive to be used must obviously be tailored to the predominant kind of work being done. However, a flexible approach must be maintained in areas where different methods of measurement and incentive types are indicated.

Environmental Factors

In addition to the six kinds of work, environmental factors, although less tangible, definitely affect the suitability of incentives of one type or another. One such factor is the total size of the enterprise. A firm with a large direct labor payroll can justifiably support a highly trained and sophisticated work measurement effort, but the plant with only a few dozen employees obviously must rely on simpler approaches to the incentive problem. Similarly, when labor cost is a large portion of the total manufacturing cost, more attention to work measurement and incentives is justified than when labor costs are a relatively minor item.

Another important factor is the type of management. To a great degree, success with wage incentives, whether new systems or modifications of old ones, will depend on an objective evaluation of the following questions:

- Is management aggressive or passive?
- Is management sales-, finance-, or production-oriented—or is there a reasonable balance of attention to all these functions?
- Is management willing to see that its incentive plans are properly administered and supported?
- Is management dedicated to a sound investment in a capable industrial engineering department?
- Is management willing to deal with the inevitable difficulties connected with any wage incentive plan?
- Is management willing to adhere to sound wage payment principles, or will it compromise those principles under industrial relations pressure?

The proper answers involve some determination of management's orientation toward either the importance of cost reduction or the industrial relations area. This evaluation may be difficult for those directly involved, but some determination must be made. Outside counsel is frequently helpful for that purpose.

Outside factors may often shape management's basic philosophy.

Interest in cost reduction is frequently related to the intensity of competition, the extent and magnitude of profit margins, and the flexibility of the price-volume relationship. Those three factors will influence management's interest in investing in a capable industrial engineering function. If an intensely competitive situation does not exist, management is frequently content with an easy-going level of manufacturing performance. Under such conditions, introduction or use of the more complicated incentive plans may be difficult and ill advised.

Management's potential interest in top performance and the use of incentives may frequently be gauged by the use of incentives in other areas: year-end bonuses, commissions for salesmen or sales incentives, and stock options as a means of encouraging top performance from the executive staff. Strong interest in these areas would indicate a disposition to consider the development of incentive plans for the labor force.

Another highly significant environmental factor is the nature of the union-management relationship. If there is deep-seated hostility on the part of the union, it certainly must be corrected before any attempt is made to introduce an incentive plan or make a major revision of an existing one. If the union-management relationship is somewhat formal and factual, simpler plans may be acceptable. On the other hand, if there is an attitude of mutual respect between labor and management and a reasonable amount of give and take in their dealings, management has a much wider choice of incentive plans and can select the plan most suited to the work done.

It is extremely difficult for management to evaluate itself specifically and objectively in many of these areas—about as difficult as it is for an individual to assess his own capabilities and weaknesses. Competent outside counsel, such as a qualified consultant familiar with incentive problems, can be extremely valuable. The consultant can make a broad objective evaluation from a frame of reference of many other companies and situations. The successful matching of incentives to the kind of work and the environment is the subject of the next chapter.

5

Fitting the Plan to the Operation

IT IS OBVIOUSLY IMPORTANT that the wage incentive plan be suited
to the kind of work being performed. A plan that is suited to highly
repetitive, standardized, short-cycle manual operations is frequently
poorly suited to work that is less structured in nature. Yet, many
industries use a single wage incentive plan regardless of its suitability
to their type of work.

Many industrial engineers also generally favor one type of incentive plan over the other. Recent surveys on the use of incentive plans
by *Factory* and other magazines have indicated that the standard-hour
plan is predominant in American industry. Presumably that has led
to its adoption in many situations where it is not completely suitable.
Most union contracts, in fact, stipulate the type of incentive plan
to be used, and among senior executives there is usually a strong
reaction in favor of one type of plan over another or daywork over
incentives in general.

Plan selection should, of course, be based on (1) the kinds and
characteristics of the wage incentives in use and the advantages and
disadvantages peculiar to each, (2) the types of work being performed and their characteristic problems of work measurement and
incentive compensation, (3) management attitudes, (4) union-management relations, and (5) industrial engineering capability. Careful

evaluation of these factors will assist in making the following preliminary determinations:[1]

1. Detailed versus average standards
2. Individual versus group incentives
3. Daily, weekly, or monthly calculations or the use of moving averages
4. The ratio for increased production versus increase in pay
5. The methods of production reporting and the need for verification of counts
6. The timekeeping effort and the correct reporting of split times
7. Administrative cost versus potential saving
8. Type of work encountered

It is unfortunate that the selection of an incentive plan is rarely based on all these preliminary determinations.

Most industries combine several of the basic types of work. For example, industries that produce standard products in large quantities will choose a plan suited to the major effort and ignore its unsuitability for relatively short run jobs, for process- or machine-controlled operations, and completely unstandardized work such as material handling, setups, maintenance, testing, shipping, and receiving.

There is good reason for industry to maintain its options in the use of wage incentives and to be able to apply the plan best suited to the specific work situation, rather than have one plan cover the entire plant. To do this effectively requires a high degree of confidence and meaningful communication between management and the employees and/or their union. The first part of this chapter will discuss the suitability of various wage plans to the different types of work in small and large plants. The second part will discuss modifications of those selections that may be dictated by environmental factors.

Standardized Repetitive Operations

OPERATIONS WITH LOW OBSOLESCENCE

This type of work usually lends itself to precise methods of measurement and also justifies the most thorough application of all of

---

[1] From a talk by H. F. Allard, Vice-President, Albert Ramond and Associates, Inc., on maintaining wage incentive plans given at the University of Wisconsin–Milwaukee, October 22, 1969.

the techniques directed toward methods improvement. The relative stability of the operations and methods generally means that methods changes and improvements will be readily identifiable. That, in turn, serves to promote prompt and accurate maintenance of the incentive structure to correspond to changes. Under those conditions an incentive plan embodying the maximum inducement to high productivity can be introduced with a minimum risk of its subsequent obsolescence. For that reason, the direct-measurement plans with 100 percent participation (straight-line type) are well suited provided there is a competent and adequate staff to carry out the necessary methods development, work measurement, auditing, and maintenance.

If, however, there are extensive process variables or variations in the quality of incoming materials, a plan with a flatter earnings-productivity ratio, such as the Halsey or Rowan plan, may be more suitable. (See Figure 1, Chapter 2). Such a plan may also be more suitable when the capacity of the staff to audit and maintain it adequately is questionable.

Sharing plans have the advantage of being able to absorb a greater amount of process or material variation without corresponding fluctuation in incentive earnings. Daywork or the various types of measured daywork are not considered suitable when it is vital to secure maximum productivity. An indirect measurement plan such as the Rucker or Scanlon plan can be used if the labor content is reasonably constant throughout the product mix. Such a plan can be used in the smaller plant, without a sizable standards staff, but its suitability to most large-scale operations is questionable.

OPERATIONS WITH MEDIUM OBSOLESCENCE

This type of work has all of the characteristics of standardized operations except for generally shorter duration of production runs. As a result, the development of methods, tooling, and operator skills will not be as refined. Standard-hour (100 percent sharing) plans are entirely suitable, but they will require considerably greater industrial engineering effort in maintenance and auditing to prevent obsolescence. The development of standard data (see Chapter 3) becomes increasingly important as a way to maintain consistency in the rate structure between various types of operations and products and to minimize the administrative costs of rate application. Smaller plants with a less than adequate industrial engineering standards staff may find the sharing plans desirable because of their smoothing tendencies.

Semistandardized Work

Semistandardized work is usually characterized by relatively short runs that often are not repeated for some interval of time. Reliance is placed on improvised tooling and methods, and so it becomes difficult to administer conventional work measurement and methods programs except to the extent that they can be applied to groups of similar items or operations that vary only in one or two major characteristics. The difficulties of measurement and administration justify the maximum use and development of standard data. The advantages of standard data—consistency and ease of application—are singularly important in such semistandardized work.

Direct-measurement straight-line plans can be used provided that complete records of methods and tooling are available for each operation and the records are maintained. There is a relatively greater potential for the development of inconsistencies because records of setup and tooling are lost or misplaced. Operator-initiated improvements that do not become a matter of record further contribute to obsolescence of the standards.

All, these work characteristics make the 100 percent plans difficult to administer. They also tend to produce wide fluctuations in earnings. The almost inevitable result is controlled production and, in some situations, banking, a well-worn shop device to average out earnings by not reporting completion of work done under extremely favorable conditions until the credits are needed to offset the lower earnings of a more difficult assignment.

Thus semistandardized work often justifies serious consideration of one of the sharing plans such as the Halsey plan with its flatter earning curve. If the established standards require a considerable amount of averaging, there is good reason to consider the use of an extended computation period. The earnings sharing plan is an application that is well suited here. (See Chapter 2 for detailed discussion.)

If relatively small employee groups, uniform labor content in the product mix, good supervision, and healthy industrial relations are present, one of the indirect plans such as the Rucker plan may also justify serious consideration. Although the appeal to maximum performance may not be as great as that of a more direct plan, the possibility of greater coverage, with application of the incentive to the entire group, may result in better overall performance and decreased total labor costs.

Unstandardized Work

Unstandardized work is represented by the typical job shop. The work done may involve contracts for specially designed products, machine repair work, or the making of tools and dies. The difficulties of accurately measuring such highly variable work ordinarily rules out plans based on conventional measurement. Attempts to improve performance over the levels realized by unmeasured daywork frequently lead to a preference for some form of measured daywork. If estimates of labor hours for the various tasks can be expected to be reasonably accurate, consideration can also be given to some of the sharing types of plans, Halsey, for example. Sharing plans ordinarily do not create the earning fluctuations that would be expected under the direct plans. As discussed in connection with semi-standardized work, a plan similar to the earnings sharing plan may offer advantages. In some instances, work measurement by multi-variant analysis such as the UniForm techniques, to be discussed in Chapter 13 and Appendix C, may be useful.

In smaller plants, if there is a relatively uniform labor content throughout the product mix and if there is mutual confidence between labor and management, serious consideration can be given to a plant-wide indirect plan such as the Rucker plan.

Process- or Mechanically Controlled Work

Most management policies today favor incentives on mechanically controlled work because earnings with incentives will then be consistent with those in other areas, facilitating transfers and avoiding grievances, and an effort to obtain optimum performance of machine or process will be encouraged. In some cases multifactor plans are very suitable; generally, they are used for specific operations. The plan may include standards for output but with modifications for such factors as material usage, yield of product, scrap factors, and machine utilization as in the Multifactor plan described in Chapter 2.

Where small groups are involved, an indirect plan such as the Rucker plan or its equivalent may be well suited. This plan is particularly advantageous when the cost of materials or related supplies is a significant factor.

Frequently process- or mechanically controlled work is accompanied by very high operating costs (overhead and expenses associated with the machine or process) and direct labor costs are a minor factor. The incentive should be designed to encourage maximum machine or process utilization. Savings in this area frequently are considerably greater than any savings due to improved labor performance. Table 3 gives an example of the cost-reduction potential of incentives on machine-controlled operators. An installation in the plant of a midwest machinery builder is also illustrative. The application involved a battery of 15 numerically controlled machining centers. Since the operations were largely tape-controlled, manual time was of little consequence. The introduction of incentives based on machine utilization resulted in an 18 to 20 percent increase in utilization, with incentive gains to the operator in the order of 13 to 15 percent over day rate.

The gain in utilization was largely the result of better operator attention, which resulted in the elimination of minor downtimes, as well as better planning by the operator for replacements of cutting tools before they became totally dull. In this particular situation, there had been a long history of increasing production requirements, and the 18 to 20 percent improvement in utilization was equivalent to the work that could have been performed by three additional machines, each valued at several hundred thousand dollars. Also, the savings in floor space in an already crowded area were significant.

One problem that frequently arises in the use of incentives when the work is largely machine-paced is the feeling on the part of many management people, as well as union people, that whenever the ma-

Table 3. Example of the cost-reduction potential of incentives on machine-controlled operations.

Machine overhead	$50.00 per hour
Direct labor	$ 3.00 per hour
Cycle time	2.00 minutes

	Assumed Machine Utilization	*Hourly Cost*	*Hourly Production*	*Unit Cost*
Non-incentive	70 %	Labor and overhead = $53.00	60.00 min ÷ 2.00 min × 70 % utilization = 21 pieces per hour	$53.00 ÷ 21 pieces = $2.52 per piece
Incentive	84 %*	Assumed 15 % incentive gain plus overhead = $3.00 × 115 % + $50.00 = $53.45	60.00 min ÷ 2.00 min × 84 % utilization = 25 pieces per hour	$53.45 ÷ 25 pieces = $2.18 per piece

* The improvement is assumed, but it is typical of numerous installations.

chine speed is increased the rate should not be reduced, the theory being that the operator works harder when the machine speed is increased. That is simply not true, because in most cases payment is made to the operator for machine attendance and it is recognized that he will not be busy throughout the entire cycle. An electronics plant in Wisconsin, which has a number of mechanized operations requiring operator attendance only, has the following policy posted in the shop:

> This rate is based on the machine speed and the operator is allowed bonus for keeping the machine fully occupied. The internal manual time shows that the operator is only ——% utilized. The company reserves the right to make use of this remaining time, either by increased machine speed or added other work without further allowance until such added work causes the manual effort to exceed the machine pace.

Work Not Measureable

"Work not measurable" refers to work that is not measurable by conventional work measurement techniques. Methods are frequently developed as the work progresses, and there is a distinct element of planning of operations and procedures. Examples would be the erection and tryout of specially designed machinery or troubleshooting on complicated equipment. Measurement of such work by conventional methods is frequently impractical. As in the case of unstandardized work, this is an area in which measurement by multivariant analyses may offer new approaches to measurement. (See UniForm, Chapter 13.)

Also in this category would be work done by crane operators, boiler room operators, watchmen, and guards. Such work does not lend itself to any type of pay plan directly related to output. In such cases, daywork is usually the only suitable plan. It is in this area that the indirect measurement plans (Rucker or Scanlon, for example) are sometimes well suited. There should, however, be a reasonably stable averaging out of the labor content in the company's production costs, and other environmental factors should also be favorable. A well-planned installation of this type can be significantly helpful in stabilizing and improving cost factors related to labor and its utilization, as well as to material usage and quality factors. Profit sharing may also be considered in the smaller organizations. However, the incentive in profit sharing is not nearly as strong as in the indirect plans. Profit sharing is not advisable if there is a history of a wide fluctuation in profit or if profits are seriously affected by factors beyond company control.

Table 4 shows the suitability of various methods of wage payment to the general types of work previously indicated for both large and small plants. The tabulation is concerned solely with the suitability of the plan itself to the various types of work. No reference has been made to the intangible factors of labor-management policy, industrial engineering capability, or prior history of wage incentives in the firm. It is therefore useful in pointing out the most desirable plan where none exists or the type of plan that might be considered in a major revision.

Environmental conditions or other intangibles may, however, dictate departures from the recommendations of Table 4. For example, an unsatisfactory history of labor-management relations within a firm would suggest a more precise plan in which all details can be mathematically accounted for. A more general type of plan, such as a Rucker plan, that is based on less tangible factors relating to overall plant performance usually requires an attitude of mutual confidence and

Table 4. Suitability of wage payment method to type of work done.

| | | Nature of Work | | | | | |
| | | Standardized and Repetitive | | | | | |
Wage Payment Method	Plant Size	Low Obsolescence	Medium Obsolescence	Semi-standardized	Unstandardized	Process or Machine Controlled	Not Measurable
Daywork	S	Poor	Weak	Weak	Usable	Good	Good
(not measured)	L	Poor	Poor	Weak	Usable	Usable	Usable
Measured daywork	S	Weak	Weak	Weak	Good	Good	Usable
	L	Poor	Poor	Weak	Good	Good	Usable
Measured daywork	S	Usable	Usable	Usable	Good	Good	Usable
with merit rating	L	Weak	Weak	Usable	Good	Usable	Poor
Direct measurement,	S	Excellent	Excellent	Good	Poor	Usable	Poor
straight-line type	L	Excellent	Excellent	Good	Poor	Usable	Poor
Direct measurement,	S	Good	Good	Good	Poor	Good	Poor
sharing type	L	Good	Good	Good	Poor	Good	Poor
Indirect measurement	S	Weak	Weak	Good	Usable	Good	Usable
—Rucker, Scanlon,	L	Weak	Weak	Weak	Usable	Good	Usable
etc.							
Profit sharing	S	Weak	Weak	Weak	Weak	Usable	Poor
	L	Poor	Poor	Poor	Poor	Poor	Poor

a generally favorable industrial relations climate with a reasonable give-and-take attitude, on the part of the involved parties. An industrial engineering or standards department with little or no experience or ability to develop sound standard data might also seriously impair the operation of a plan based largely on direct measurement of semi-standardized operations. Therefore, Table 4 should be considered largely as a general guide and a point of reference for additional study.

Administrative Factors

Practically every industrial enterprise will include many or possibly all of the various categories of work previously discussed. Therefore, the selection of a single incentive plan for the entire plant may result in either low coverage or an attempt to use the plan in areas for which it is not suitable. An incentive plan that covers only a small proportion of the hourly labor is seriously limited in its effectiveness and frequently leads to problems in the transfer of employees between incentive and non-incentive work.

Another byproduct of low incentive coverage is the request by groups of non-incentive workers for some form of incentive pay to bring their earnings up to the level of those on incentive. The request is natural and understandable, but some of the attempts to solve the problem have been disastrous because of their effect on the basic plan; an example is the payment of average incentive earnings or a fraction of them to all non-incentive workers. Since the installation is usually characterized by very little control of indirect or non-incentive labor, the usual result is to pay incentive wages for non-incentive work to a significant segment of the work force. That is simply payment of a "bonus" for which no corresponding effort has been expended, and the frequent consequence is an overall increase in labor cost despite the incentive system. The unmerited bonus completely dilutes the effect of the basic plan and often leads to a concerted effort to obtain incentive rates that will permit higher and higher earning levels and thus violate the basic principle that incentives should be earned and not guaranteed.

Another attempt to solve the problem is to pay "average earnings" to incentive workers when they are assigned to non-incentive work. This again increases the costs of unmeasured work without any corresponding increase in performance and has all the negative characteristics of the other method. The problems will be discussed in more detail in Chapter 10, "Restrictive Factors in Plan Operation."

It bears repeating that, since each of the basic types of incentive plans is suited to specific categories of work, the adoption of a single plan for an entire plant will result in either low coverage or difficulties of administration in plant areas to which the plan is not too well adapted. The preferred alternative is to select and design individual plans based on the specific characteristics of individual work centers or departments. That can represent a real challenge to the industrial engineering department as well as give a new outlook to the typical union-management relationship based on dealing with a single incentive plan for the entire plant.

It is a fact of industrial life today that all incentive plans or modifications to them are subject to union-management negotiation. Even in the absence of a union it is necessary to gain employee acceptance and understanding if a wage plan is to succeed. The existence of a union generally formalizes the necessary communication and discussion. That presents a real opportunity to the management team, since objective discussions with union representatives can often improve employee understanding and acceptance of proposed installations of or modifications in wage incentives.

The discussion approach to solving the problems related to wage incentives has considerable potential. Although much depends on the personalities involved, members of the union-management committee frequently make valuable contributions. One important point is that the committee should confine itself to a constructive approach to joint solution of broad wage incentive policies. The employee members of such a committee constitute a valuable source of feedback to management on shop situations that might otherwise go unrecognized.

The committee should never become involved in specific grievances or in collective bargaining problems. If it does not separate itself from those efforts, the entire group will lose its objectivity. The value of such a committee lies in the fact that neither party is trying to win an argument or bargain on contract details but is instead confining itself to solving mutual problems and improving the wage incentive climate. Often the presence of a third party who is impartial but well versed in the problem, such as the management consultant, facilitates the work of the committee. The third party frequently develops the agenda for the meeting and, by means of informal and off-the-record discussions with various members of the committee can frequently make worthwhile suggestions without having them appear to be either management- or union-oriented.

The general climate of the management-employee relationship is an important consideration in selecting an incentive plan. If the relationship has been rigid and formal and all grievances relating to incentives have been settled on a strictly factual and mathematical basis, a transition to some of the sharing plans or indirect plans, which will necessarily involve considerable averaging of conditions, may be somewhat difficult to accomplish. Such plans are more suitable where there is an atmosphere of mutual confidence and respect and both management and its employees have a give-and-take attitude. That is particularly true of the Rucker and Scanlon plans, which necessarily involve publication and interpretation of the concern's operating figures.

The capability of the industrial engineering function must also be considered. As the industrial engineering activity extends itself beyond the conventional time study and measurement procedures used in developing direct standards, there is an increasing requirement for use of the newer techniques, such as work sampling, group time study and the newer statistical approaches, for developing data with assured confidence levels. Thus, changes in or additions to existing incentive systems certainly require extensive evaluation of the capabilities of the industrial engineering function within the plant. This point will be covered in Chapter 7.

Broad coverage through the use of plantwide incentive plans does present management with certain options. If it is practical to develop a broad coverage of most of the labor in a plant (direct and indirect) by the use of straight-line or sharing plans, the appeal to maximum output may develop optimum overall cost reduction potentials. On the other hand, if coverage by such a plan is limited by the nature of the work being done, then the use of the indirect plans may be a suitable alternative; the fact that all employees can be placed on the plan instead of only a portion may result in the best overall cost reductions even though the incentive appeal to the individual is not as great as under the direct plans.

There is a third alternative that may be quite practical in a number of cases: the use of direct incentives, either straight-line or sharing, in the portion of the work that is suited to such plans and the use of one or the other of the indirect plans for the remaining portion of the work (either unstandardized or indirect labor).

Thus the indirect plans can be used as a substitute for the direct plans in certain areas, or it may be feasible to apply them on a plantwide basis. In that case, production workers covered by direct incentives could also share in the earnings accruing to all workers by reason of the plantwide incentive. Installations of this type require careful analysis by experienced professionals.

6

Evaluating the Existing Plan

Whether a wage incentive plan is operating as effectively as it should is seldom determinable by ordinary factory control accounting, which usually indicates departmental and plantwide averages of incentive gains and incentive coverage. As long as those averages are reasonably consistent with historical patterns in the plant, top management usually assumes that the incentive system is performing as expected. Because of that complacent assumption, a number of significant and often inconspicuous indicators are frequently overlooked. Averages of incentive gains do not indicate the range of variation, nor do they show whether or not the actual distribution of incentive gains on both sides of the average approaches the normal distribution curve.

Measurement of Coverage

Conventional accounting methods that show incentive coverage may also be meaningless in the absence of effective labor utilization and accurate control of the timekeeping function. Certain indirect accounts such as factory excess labor (lost time, waiting for material or work assignments, machine repairs, tool repairs, salvage, and rework) or factory support accounts (material handling, setup, maintenance, and inspection) are frequently misused. They may be used as adjusting devices to maintain incentive earnings at some desired level or to absorb excess man-hours resulting from improved performance under incentives. This will be discussed in more detail in Chapter 8, "The Shop Administration Factor."

With lack of control in indirect accounts, coverage may actually show a decrease even though all known standard work in the department has been measured and is being done under incentives. In the extreme cases, such practices may actually result in an increase in total labor costs. Standard measured work is paid for at incentive rates, but with poor controls, indirect accounts may be used either to absorb surplus labor or to control incentive gains at some desired level. This type of situation is illustrated by the example of the Super Garden Tractor before and after the installation of incentives. The company is hypothetical and the figures are contrived, but not unusual.

EXAMPLE. The Super Garden Tractor Company employed approximately 60 hourly employees who worked 10,000 hours per month for an average of $3 per hour before the incentive installation. Output is marketed through a sales organization which consistently requires approximately 200 tractors a month. In an effort to reduce costs the company discussed the situation with several consulting firms and selected one that was qualified in the field of work measurement and wage incentive installation. After a preliminary survey the consultant reported that operations and methods were quite well standardized and that the operation appeared to be suitable for the installation of a direct measurement wage incentive plan. Consequently, time studies were taken and standards were developed and a standard-hour wage incentive plan was installed for all of the workers on direct operations.

Condition 1 of the factory operating statement outlines the basic statistics of manufacturing before the installation of the incentive plan. Direct operations required 6000 hours. That level of production required about 2500 hours of support labor (indirect) including setups, material handling, inspection, and tool grinding. Another 1500 hours of excess labor (also indirect) consisted of repairs, rework, waiting for materials, and lost time. The total of all labor hours, then, was 10,000 per month.

Condition 2 shows how the same labor statistics could develop after incentive installation but under conditions of poor labor control. The superintendent, E. C. Goeing, had been in his position for twenty years. He felt that his experience qualified him to judge how many men it would take to operate his department for a given output. He had little faith in incentives and believed firmly in stabilized employment situations. His superiors in management took little interest in effective labor controls, and he was furnished with very little information on which to plan his utilization of manpower.

FACTORY OPERATING STATEMENT

	Condition 1	Condition 2	Condition 3
1. Number of tractors produced	200	200	200
2. Total hours—direct operators	6,000	4,000	4,000
3. Earned hours on incentive	—	4,800	4,800
4. Total hours of support labor (setup, material handling, inspection, tool grinding)	2,500	3,000	2,500
5. Total hours of excess labor (repairs, rework, waiting for material, lost time)	1,500	3,000	1,500
6. Total labor hours:			
Actual, a (items 2, 4, 5)*	10,000	10,000	8,000
Standard, b (items 3, 4, 5)†	—	10,800	8,800
Statistics			
7. Total hours per tractor, item 6 (a or b) ÷ item 1	50	54	44
8. Labor cost per tractor, item 7 × \$3.00	\$150	\$162	\$132
9. Incentive gain, (item 3 ÷ item 2) × 100	—	120%	120%
10. Incentive coverage, (item 2 ÷ item 6a) × 100	—	40%	50%
11. Factory support ratio, item 4 ÷ item 2	.42	.75	.63
12. Factory excess ratio, item 5 ÷ item 2	.25	.75	.38

* Daywork   † Incentive

After installation of incentives, Goeing's men began to increase their output and achieved satisfactory incentive earnings. However, within a short time they were ahead of schedule and parts shortages began to develop. Not having realized that his parts supply schedule was geared to a relatively constant production of 200 tractors per month, Goeing began to try to find other work for his men during their periods of waiting for material. The assignments were largely unplanned. Depending entirely on the momentary situation, he would put his men on inspection, rework, material handling, or tool grinding or simply tell them to punch out on waiting for material or for lost time.

As a result, the total hours for support labor increased from 2500 per month to 3000 per month and the excess labor hours increased from 1500 per month to approximately 3000 per month. Goeing had merely succeeded in diverting his surplus labor to uncontrolled accounts and had maintained his work force at the 60 employees customarily assigned to his department. However, he was now paying incentive earnings to his employees on direct work, so that he was actually paying out 10,800 hours (earned hours plus daywork) instead of the original 10,000. The net result was that the total hours per tractor increased from 50 to 54 and the total labor cost per tractor increased from $150 to $162 in spite of incentives. Goeing became more and more irritated with his attempts to keep his men busy and began to blame the lost time and parts shortages on the poor production control.

In the meantime, the accounting department in reviewing his operating figures brought to management's attention the fact that, in spite of incentives, unit labor costs had increased from $150 to $162. After reviewing the figures presented by the accounting department and discussing the situation with Goeing, management concluded that the installation of the incentive plan had been a mistake and that it was costing money and bitterly regretted the consulting fees paid out for installation of the plan. They firmly resolved to eliminate the incentive plan at the next contract negotiation with their union.

In condition 3, with the same original' statistics, the installation of incentives was accomplished with the use of effective labor controls and good management techniques. Here the superintendent, A. Stute, had worked in close collaboration with his top management to develop effective labor controls and carefully reviewed the monthly operating statements given him by the accounting department. He noted that prior to installation of incentives his department effectively produced 200 tractors per month with approximately 2500 hours of factory support labor and 1500 hours of excess labor and felt that those ratios could be maintained regardless of incentive performance by the direct operators.

He reasoned that the increased performance under an incentive plan would permit the same output of tractors with fewer man-hours, and he planned his manpower loading to meet that situation. He did so largely by not replacing people who left his employ, by carefully weeding out doubtful probationary employees, and by transferring excess labor to other departments whenever possible. As a result of his plan he was able to eliminate 2000 hours from his department. He did so by maintaining total hours of factory support labor at previous levels of 2500 and total hours of excess labor at prevous levels of 1500.

Thus, in Stute's situation the installation of incentives plus careful manpower controls reduced the total hours per tractor from 50 hours to 44 and reduced the labor costs per tractor from $150 to $132, a savings of $3600 per month or approximately $44,000 annually in labor costs. Management was well satisfied with the program and contemplated extending incentive coverage to other areas.

These two different outcomes point out clearly the importance of the factory support and factory excess ratio controls. Note that under Goeing's administration the factory support jumped from .42 to .75 and the factory excess ratio from .25 to .75 merely because of careless assignment of men to those indirect operations. Under Stute's administration, the same ratios increased from .42 to .63 in the case of the support ratio and from .25 to .38 for the factory excess ratio. However, the increases are only apparent, for they are due to the smaller number of direct hours used as a denominator. Under the incentive plan these new ratios would form a new standard of performances.

Incentive Coverage

Another yardstick that is frequently used to measure the performance of the industrial engineering function is incentive coverage. If that coverage drops for any reason, the usual implied criticism is that the industrial engineering or standards department is not performing its function. Actually, under inadequate controls, the apparent coverage may drop, with resultant criticism of the standards people, when in reality all measurable work in a department or work center may be done on incentives. A more proper definition of coverage would be the total amount of direct labor performed on incentives divided by total *direct* labor in the department. That would include work on incentives as well as direct labor performed under daywork conditions.

FACTORY EXCESS AND SUPPORT RATIOS

A preferred method of controlling indirect labor is to divide the chart of accounts into two categories: factory excess and factory support as in the Super Garden Tractor example. Both accounts are production-related and can be considered as variables. Factory excess accounts are considered to be those activities incurred as a result of less than ideal shop performance. They would normally include such items as time lost in waiting for material or a crane, lost time due to machine or tool breakdowns, and time spent on salvage and rework. If labor hours for all these and similar functions are totaled for each accounting period and the result is divided by the total hours spent on standard direct operations (actual hours on incentives), the resulting index becomes a highly sensitive tool for measuring the effectiveness of labor utilization and accuracy of timekeeping.

In like manner, factory support accounts, normally including such items as material handling, setup, maintenance and repairs, and hourly inspection, when totaled and again divided by actual hours on incentive, produce an equally valuable index for determining how effectively the support operations are controlled.

FACTORY OPERATING STATEMENT

Table 5 represents a typical factory operating statement with an arrangement of account numbers similar to those in most manufacturing charts of accounts. Values are expressed in hours, although dollars can be used. The plan presupposes a standard-hour incentive plan in which the incentive is expressed in standard hours per unit of output. The arrangement also illustrates the adaptability of the standard-hour plan as a control device for labor utilization, as pointed out in Chapter 2. For the four months represented, January to April, the total work force remained relatively constant at between 36,000 and 37,000 total hours (line 17).

Production schedules remained fairly constant through January, February, and March (line 1) but decreased from approximately 19,000 hours to 16,700 hours from March to April. The number of actual hours on standard (line 2) decreased in about the same proportion. As a result, the usual control figures for incentive gains and coverage (lines a and b under controls) were not significantly affected. Note that incentive gains showed the normal variation between 123 and 127 percent and incentive coverage varied between 84 and 87 percent. These minor fluctuations in themselves would not ordinarily call for serious investigation, particularly since the total of all hours of labor remained relatively constant between 36,000 and 37,000 hours per month.

Two other indices, however, indicate serious problems in control and utilization of indirect labor. The factory excess index, line c, is a total of downtime for various reasons plus salvage and rework divided by standard hours produced. It shows that, for every standard hour produced, between .14 and .16 hour were spent on excess accounts in January, February, and March and .202 hour were spent in April, when there was a significant decrease in scheduled production.

Factory support accounts showed the same upward trend. The factory support index, line d, covering material handling, setups, and maintenance and repairs divided by standard hours produced, shows that .42 hour of factory support labor were required for every hour of standard production in January. The amount increased quite consistently to a value of .69 during April. The increase of 55 percent over four months indicates a serious lack of control of indirect labor.

Indices c and d are highly sensitive ways of measuring how

Table 5. Typical factory operating statement: payroll analysis in hours.

	January	February	March	April
DIRECT LABOR				
1. Standard hours produced	19,701	19,317	19,611	16,714
2. Actual hours on standard	16,062	15,282	15,793	13,341
3. Direct labor on daywork	3,010	2,830	2,390	1,990
4. Total direct labor hours	19,072	18,112	18,183	15,331
INDIRECT LABOR				
5. Downtime, no schedule	263	153	169	193
6. Downtime, machine repairs	1,332	1,298	1,200	1,210
7. Downtime, tool repairs	160	280	317	143
8. Downtime, waiting for material	281	317	481	592
9. Material handling	3,140	4,004	3,703	4,578
10. Setup	1,240	960	1,070	1,385
11. Maintenance and repair	3,890	4,273	5,285	5,592
12. Salvage and rework	860	925	1,017	1,230
13. Hourly supervision	1,614	1,623	1,582	1,618
14. Hourly inspection	2,912	2,765	2,843	2,845
15. Factory clerical	1,369	1,394	1,463	1,411
16. Total indirect labor	17,061	17,987	19,130	20,797
17. Total all labor	36,133	37,099	37,313	36,128
CONTROLS				
a. Incentive gain, (1) ÷ (2) × 100	123%	127%	124%	125%
b. Incentive coverage, (2) ÷ (4) × 100	84%	84%	87%	87%
c. Factory excess index [(5) + (6) + (7) + (8) + (12)] ÷ (1)	.147	.155	.148	.202
d. Factory support index [(9) + (10) + (11)] ÷ (1)	.420	.475	.540	.69

effectively indirect operations are maintained in proper ratio to the work load in the plant or department. Their use in conjunction with a wage incentive installation rests on the fact that they measure shop administration in two areas: (1) the tendency to transfer to indirect areas the surplus labor created by the increase in productivity due to an incentive system and (2) the tendency of shop supervision to use either excess or factory support accounts as a device for artificially controlling or enhancing incentive earnings.

Pressure by management for high levels of incentive coverage produces many undesirable side effects. The pressure to apply incentives to every new operation, and the corollary relegation of correct methods to secondary consideration, inevitably results in many poor methods and the permanent freezing of the excess time resulting from untried operations into the incentive structure. Under extreme pressure, time study men are too frequently prone to merely time-study an operation and establish a rate rather than take the time necessary to establish a correct method and see that the operator is trained in that method before attempting to establish the standard. The important function of developing standard data is then completely neglected.

Pressure on the time study man is too often in the direction of "let's get a rate on this job in a hurry so that we can start getting out the production." The complete evaluation of the performance of an incentive system requires a great deal of careful investigation beyond the mere analysis of incentive gains and coverage, since those two figures are in themselves highly unreliable. The techniques to be described in the rest of this chapter are intended for use in evaluating all aspects of the plan's performance as well as pointing out areas in which corrective action is needed. Such action may be directed toward improving shop administration or it may require improved effectiveness of the industrial engineering function. The suitability of the plan to the work being performed must also be evaluated.

SHOP OBSERVATIONS

Following a review of the overall statistics of coverage and incentive earnings, the audit should proceed to shop level for further subjective checking. Heading the list would be a number of shop tours at irregular intervals and unannounced times. During such a tour a trained observer can readily note many important indicators:

- A judgment of the overall work pace and levels of performance as related to indicated levels of incentive gains.
- The relative amounts of visiting.
- Observed idleness or aimless walking.
- Levels of activity shortly before the end of the shift. (This is particularly significant.)

An excessive number of employees obviously idle or engaged in aimless cleanup or report writing 15 to 20 minutes before the end of the shift usually indicates laxity in shop administration and is frequently symptomatic of a loose incentive structure. A rough form of sampling is a walking tour at irregular intervals through all departments of the plant while merely counting the number of idle employees observed. In one period, during which an entire wage incentive structure was being revised, a fairly significant relationship was thereby noted. The number of idle employees decreased in proportion to the improved performance and installation of the revised incentive. The observed relationship may not have been statistically reliable, but it did provide a rough yardstick for measuring generally improved output.

WORKING RELATIONSHIPS

The working relationship between the line foremen and the representatives of the standards department is extremely important. Interviews and discussions with the foremen and with the various time study men will usually show whether the relationship is cooperative, satisfactory, and based on mutual respect. It is in this area that the attitude of top management toward incentives and its administration of those policies becomes extremely important. Serious problems can arise if the respective functions of the time study man and the foreman are not clearly defined, understood, and practiced. For example, is the ultimate responsibility for selection of proper methods assigned to the foreman, to the industrial engineer, or to both of them as a joint effort or is it a wide-open area? Does the foreman support the incentive plan in his dealings with his people, or does he consider it as a necessary evil? His attitude in this respect will be largely a reflection of top management's attitude. Are communications between foreman and time study man on a level of mutual respect and recognition of the fact that each is in a position to make major contributions? Personality clashes between foremen and time study men may exist, but the effect can be minimized with proper organizational direction.

SUPERVISORY ATTITUDES

Discussions with the foremen should also be aimed at studying the manner and effectiveness of reporting methods changes. Questioning should be directed towards verification of the following items:

- Are simple improvements—either employee-initiated or management-initiated—promptly reported to the standards department so that the standards can be revised immediately?
- Are operator-initiated improvements and gadgets considered the personal property of the employee?
- Are there definite policies for properly adjusting rates when simple improvements are made?
- Is there a formalized recognition of the employee's contribution toward improved output?
- Are definite procedures established for the reporting of improvements, or is the reporting dependent on the momentary whims of the foreman or occasional policing by standards personnel?

Conversations with individual employees will frequently bring out conditions that may impair the proper functioning of the incentive plan, such as inadequate production control, incorrect route sheets, inadequate or improper tooling, and improper maintenance of productive equipment. Assembly work, for example, may be seriously hampered by parts shortages or poor quality of components from another department. If those factors are not included in the rate, dissatisfaction with the incentive and poor performance levels will result. If they are included, there is a very great probability that the standards will be too loose after corrective measures have been taken in other areas.

REVIEW OF SHOP LABOR TICKETS

Malfunctioning of the incentive plan can frequently be detected in a sample review of shop labor tickets. A reasonable sampling might include one day of tickets in a medium-size shop or several hundred tickets selected from various departments in a larger organization. The tickets should be reviewed to form a background of the following information:

- The average duration of the job.
- The manner in which setups, lost time, and so on are accounted for (by punch-outs or foreman approval, for example).
- The extent of split time (alternate punching between daywork and incentive jobs).
- Accuracy of rate application and whether correct rates are used.

• Whether setups and operation numbers are validated by route sheets or similar documents.

Whenever the amount of split time is substantial, it is a serious detriment to the success of the wage incentive plan. The solution may be:

• Analysis of the type of work being done on a daywork basis. Probably some of the areas are measurable and can be placed on incentives.
• Reassignment of some daywork operations to people who are not classed as incentive operators.
• Installation of an indirect group plan that includes all labor within the department or work center.

Labor tickets should also be examined for possible alteration of rates by a foreman. Records should be examined for questionable additions for daywork or material handling to direct labor on incentives. They should also be checked for operations for which rates are in existence but were not applied for one reason or another. Posted quantities of finished work must be audited against production records of related operations and by inspector's counts.

TRENDS OF INCENTIVE GAINS

When the information is available, it is worthwhile to plot a graph of incentive performance for several preceding years such as the one in Figure 7. An incentive system that is under control will show normal fluctuations above and below the expected level of incentive gains as in curve (*a*), "normal variations in incentive gain." If there are no substantial variations, rigged performance or controlled production levels can be presumed to exist. That condition is indicated by curve (*b*), "controlled performance." Rigged performance can often be verified by constructing earning distribution curves for various departments or work centers; this will be discussed in the next section.

A pronounced upward trend of incentive gains (as in curve (*c*) of Figure 7, "runaway incentive plan") over a several-year period is symptomatic of a runaway incentive plan or one that is not being maintained. Without good audit procedures, creeping changes will gradually loosen any incentive structure. In many cases, particularly when a union is aggressive or management is overly sympathetic to employee complaints, the tendency is to adjust tight rates on the basis of complaints or grievances and in disregard of time study data or the merits of the situation. The result is that most rates that show earnings less than accepted averages are loosened up. Since there are never any complaints about standards that are too loose, the trend is toward a complete relaxing of the entire rate structure and an increase of average earnings without corresponding improvements in performance.

In such an environment, the average industrial engineering or standards department is faced with the extremely difficult task of

Figure 7. Typical incentive performances.

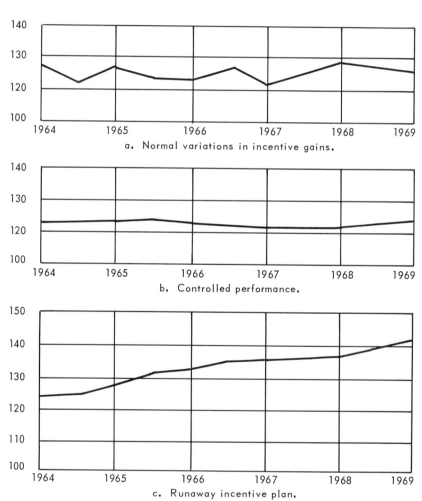

a. Normal variations in incentive gains.

b. Controlled performance.

c. Runaway incentive plan.

maintaining the proper relationship between published standards and the work content of the operations they represent. Fortunately, in many of these situations parts or product obsolescence comes to the rescue.

In a large plant, curves of the type shown in Figure 7 should be developed for each major department, and most standards departments will maintain them for both major departments and the entire plant as a normal procedure. The information is exceptionally valuable in analyzing the long-term trend of the incentive plan.

Distribution of Incentive Gains

Profiles showing the distribution patterns of incentive gains are an excellent device for analyzing and studying the functioning or malfunctioning of the incentive plan. The profiles can easily be developed from conventional payroll records. Numerous well-documented statistical studies have established that the output of a large number of workers will range from minimum to maximum in the ratio of approximately 1:2.25, or from a low of about 60 percent of average

Figure 8. Output of 1,000 random people.

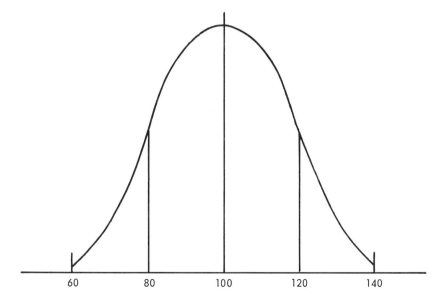

| 60 | 80 | 100 | 120 | 140 |

production to a high of approximately 140 percent. The largest number of performances will cluster around the average, or 100 percent mark, and a normal distribution will produce the familiar bell-shaped performance distributions curve illustrated in Figure 8.

Under an incentive system that is functioning well, a normal distribution of incentive earnings will usually follow the general shape of the curve shown in Figure 9, where the peak has been shifted to the right by about 20 or 25 percent points to coincide with expected incentive gains. Under ideal conditions (performance at high task levels and good operator motivation), there may even be a greater proportion of above-normal earnings. Assuming that the rate structure is technically sound and truly representative of the work content of the various jobs throughout the shop, a distribution of this type would indicate good motivation toward the incentive plan as well as the probable action of a secondary factor: substandard workers are either eliminated, transferred, or made the object of more super-

Figure 9. Normal distribution of incentive gains.

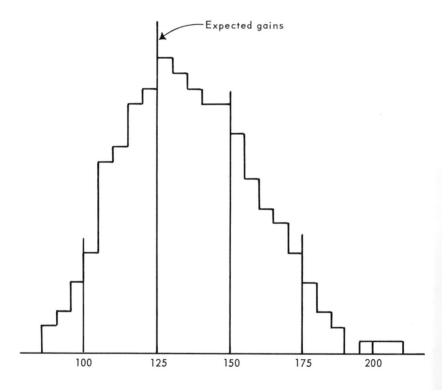

Figure 10. Actual distribution of incentive gains.

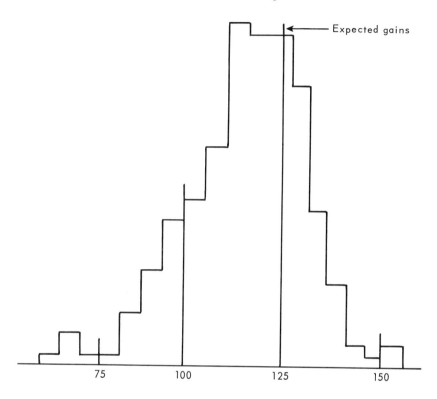

Figure 11. Effect of variation in materials or methods on incentive gain distribution.

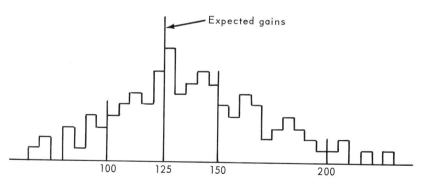

visory attention, while superior workers are encouraged to stay because of higher-than-normal earning potentials.

It is rather unusual for a distribution of actual performance to
follow the normal distribution precisely. Figure 10 shows a curve
developed from actual performance in the plant of a midwest
machinery builder that approaches the normal curve quite well. However, in most cases there are some variations due to external conditions
such as morale factors, variations in shop methods, or perhaps the
mathematics of the incentive plan itself.

Care must be exercised in analyzing such distributions. Two major
factors may prevent a normal distribution. One is a preponderance
of group operations in which all employees pool their incentive gains.

Figure 12. Wide distribution of Figure 11 recalculated to show effect of Halsey 50-50 plan.

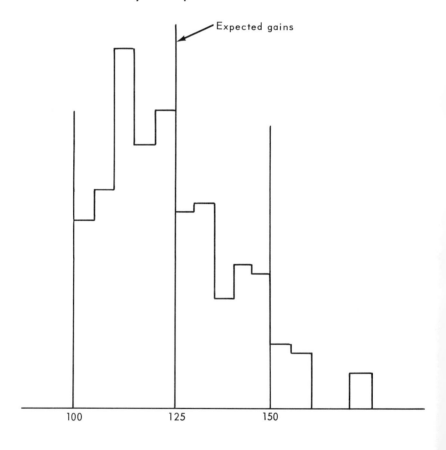

The result is a single earning level for a large group, which obviously will conceal a normal distribution. The other factor is a high percentage of machine- or process-controlled operations. Both factors will develop relatively constant incentive gains instead of the normal variations and produce a truncated distribution instead of the normal curve.

If the nature of the work being done is such that there is considerable variation in material or if methods have not been well standardized, introduction of the additional variables will frequently develop a distribution curve like that shown in Figure 11, and particularly so if a standard-hour incentive (1:1) is used. In such cases the use of one of the sharing plans such as the Halsey 50-50 or the Rowan will have the effect of narrowing the extreme range of incentive gains and will develop a more satisfactory distribution pattern. Figure 12 is based on performance distribution identical with that of Figure 11 but recalculated to reflect the actual earnings distribution of a Halsey 50-50 plan. Note the reduction in the amounts of unusually high earnings as well as the increased proportion in the lower performance ranges. The rearrangement is typical of the Halsey plan, which admittedly penalizes superior performance and enhances incentive gains for mediocre output.

When the entire incentive policy is loosely administered, or when there has been poor maintenance of the plan, or when the level of performance rating has been too liberal, the distribution curve may very likely shift to the right as shown in Figure 13. A distribution of this type invites a careful examination of time study procedures and leveling techniques used in the industrial engineering or standards department. This topic will be taken up in the following chapter.

Figure 14 shows incentive earnings that fall within an extremely narrow range. Diagnosis here points to an incentive structure that is so loose or liberal that even substandard operators can achieve satisfactory earnings combined with limitation of production to some level informally adopted by the employees or imposed by social pressures or union philosophy. Remedial action is more complicated and involves, first, careful study of the industrial engineering or standards department with a view to eliminating poor practices and, second, finding ways to motivate employees to optimum performance levels. The second action may involve a carefully thought out educational program and, in many cases, frank and objective discussions with the union representatives. Sometimes the plan may be so outmoded that complete replacement is the only answer.

Figure 13. Effect of loose standards or leveling on incentive gain distribution.

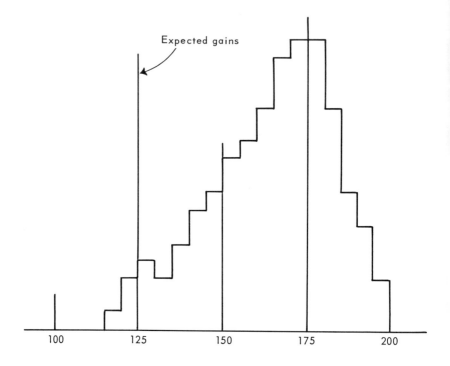

The distribution of Figure 14 is not unusual. In a survey of incentive earnings in a number of industrial plants in southeastern Wisconsin about 50 percent of the plants developed that pattern; an actual profile typical of that group is shown in Figure 15. Occasionally, lack of motivation, lack of confidence in the incentive plan, or a feeling that it is impossible to attain satisfactory incentive gains will result in a curve similar to that shown in Figure 16. Many times the reasons for poor performance are quite obscure, and the conventionally stated reasons, such as "rates too tight," seldom reveal the true cause. A careful investigation must be made to find out what is really happening, and it may require such techniques as group time studies or work sampling, which frequently will reveal many contributing factors. An example of methods of auditing this type of problem is discussed in more detail in Chapter 8.

AUDIT OF PLAN AND ADMINISTRATION

The various conditions referred to can be used to develop a standardized checklist for the operational auditing of the wage incentive plan and its administration within the shop. The following points should be noted:.

1. What are the levels of incentive gain and coverage, both departmental and plantwide?
2. Is excess labor that results from the greater productivity of the incentive plan being directed to non-incentive supporting services?
3. Is there evidence of undue pressure for coverage before adequate standardization of proper methods and operator training?

Figure 14. Effect of controlled earnings on incentive gain distribution.

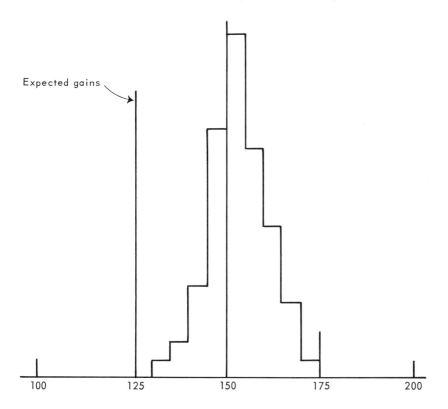

Figure 15. Actual example of the effect of controlled earnings on incentive gain distribution.

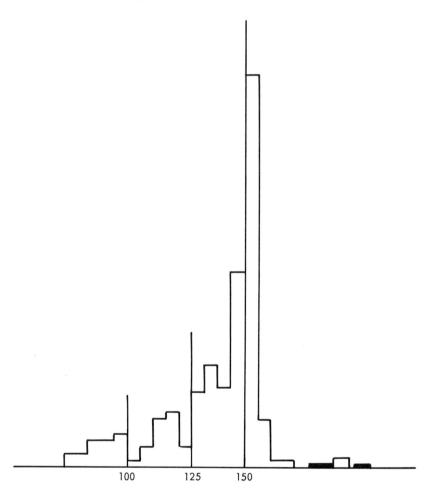

4. Are work pace and performance consistent with incentive earnings?
5. Are there indications of excess idleness during the day, and especially before shift changes?
6. What is the attitude of foreman and employees toward the incentive plan?
7. What are the attitudes of the union toward the incentives?
8. What are the procedures and attitudes toward prompt reporting of methods changes, however slight?

9. Are labor tickets being audited on the basis of representative samples? The points to cover in such an audit are:

Length of job
Proper accounting for time spent on setups, material handling, and delays
Split time
Evidence of unauthorized rate by foreman or others
Evidence of improper allowances being added to the incentives
Evidence that existing rates are not being applied for one reason or another
Adequate verification of counts and quantities turned in

10. What are the long-term trends in incentive gains, both departmental and plantwide?
11. Do either departmental or plantwide earning profiles indicate unsatisfactory distributions?

Figure 16. Effect of lack of incentive effort on incentive gain distribution.

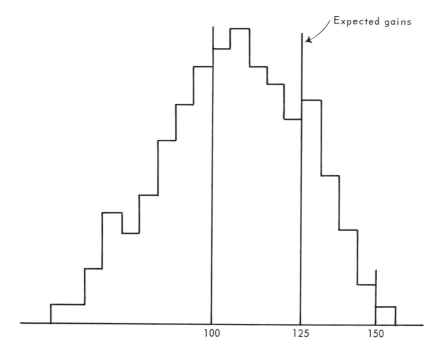

Figure 17. Checklist for audit of wage incentive plan.

PLANT_____ DEPARTMENT_____ DATE_____

Item	Very Good	Good	Normal	Unsat-isfac-tory	Needs help
1. Incentive gains					
2. Incentive coverage					
3. Excessive non-incentive allowances					
4. Evidence of pressure for coverage					
5. Work pace					
6. Excess idleness					
7. Foreman attitudes					
8. Employee attitudes					
9. Union attitudes					
10. Reporting of methods changes					
11. Sampling of labor tickets:					
a. Average length of job					
b. Handling of non-incentive time					
c. Extent of split time					
d. Unauthorized rate alterations					
e. Unauthorized allowances					
f. Rates not used					
g. Verification of counts					
12. Long term earning trends					
13. Incentive earning profiles					

14. Other comments: _____

_____

Audit by _____

Figure 17 illustrates a simple form that has been developed to record observations made during an audit.

7

The Industrial Engineering Function

THE SPECIFIC RESPONSIBILITIES assigned to the industrial engineering or standards department will vary widely between individual plants and industries. The popular conception of responsibility for work measurement, work methods, and wage incentive administration is generally accurate; those functions have always accounted for a large proportion of the industrial engineering effort. However, many other functions are now frequently assigned to the industrial engineering department:

Production engineering
Manufacturing analysis and control
Facilities planning
Safety
Production and inventory planning
Quality control
Plant engineering
Operations research
Handling of grievance procedures
Assistance with collective bargaining
Cost estimating of new products or quotations

Thus, the industrial engineering department is becoming involved with an increasing number of the engineering-related functions of manufacturing. The implementation of the newer management techniques becomes a logical assignment for the department, and frequently such responsibilities as operations research, program evaluation and review techniques (PERT), critical path methods, computer programming, and systems and procedures research are assigned to it. That may be a highly favorable development, but it imposes upon the department a requirement for many of the newer skills that have served to elevate its function from the purely technical to the highly professional level. In addition, the increasing involvement of employees and employee representatives in problems related to the wage incentive function have required of the industrial engineer a high development of social skills and communications abilities.

The requirement for increased sophistication on the part of the industrial engineer makes a degree in industrial engineering from a recognized college or university highly desirable. However, successful application of the newer techniques to specific manufacturing problems also requires extensive practical knowledge and experience with specific manufacturing processes. The ideal industrial engineering department, therefore, should combine strength in both areas: a careful balance of the professionally educated engineer and the shop-trained practitioner. Each can profit from the contributions of the other.

In this chapter, evaluation of the industrial engineering function will be confined to a review of activity in work measurement, work design, and wage incentive administration. Included will be an analysis of time study and related work measurement, improvement and standardization of methods, and the development of effective standard data.

Time Study

Proponents of predetermined time systems, such as MTM, work factor, and master standard data, have predicted at various times that the stopwatch and conventional forms of time study will become obsolete. Certainly predetermined time procedures are being successfully used in an ever-increasing number of applications. However, conventional stopwatch time study is still the predominant method for work measurement in industrial use today. In some areas it will continue to be the only practical means of work measurement. A

1969 survey* of 39 reporting companies found that:

- Nine (23 percent) set standards by use of the stopwatch at least 65 percent of the time.
- Sixteen (41 percent) set standards by use of standard data at least 65 percent of the time.
- Three (8 percent) set standards by use of synthetic time values at least 65 percent of the time.
- Ten (26 percent) set standards by use of a combination of methods.
- One uses historical data to set standards 100 percent of the time.

Conventional methods are also used to measure process times and verify machine-controlled times, although the latter can often be reduced to a formula.

It is, then, difficult to overemphasize the importance of carefully made and well-documented time studies. They are just as much engineering documents as blueprints are, and they should be prepared just as carefully. They frequently constitute the only record of work methods and their time values as they existed at the time of the study. Since most union grievances involving incentive rates are based on data and evidence obtained from time studies, the time studies themselves usually become exhibits in the grievance procedure. All this adds to the importance of maintaining time study files that are legible, neat, and easily understood so they can be used as convincing documentary evidence.

The quality and degree of standard data development is another important criterion in measuring the effectiveness and competence of the standards function. Up to the present time a large portion of existing standard data have been based on time studies, although data developed from predetermined time systems are assuming increasing importance. More recently, computer-based standard data developed by such methods as UnivEl and UniForm—to be discussed in Chapter 13—show great promise in ultimately substituting for much conventional time study. However, the methods are highly sophisticated and require the use of trained technicians and computer availability, so their adoption will be evolutionary. Therefore, the effectiveness of the industrial engineering standard will be judged by the quality of its time study techniques and its standard data development for some time to come.

* By the Milwaukee Chapter, Society for Advancement of Management.

Unfortunately, very few existing rate files are exemplary. Far too many files contain sloppily filled out forms with various untitled multiplications and factorings, ambiguous descriptions of work elements, and incomplete notations. They are not impressive documents to present to a union time study steward or to an impartial arbitrator or fact finder, although all time studies should be prepared with the possibility of that ultimate destination in mind. Another point to remember is that, at the time the study is taken, many details of an operation are fresh and vivid in the mind of the observer and other persons on the standards staff. With the passage of time, memory becomes unreliable and the documentary information on the study is all that is available.

Evaluation of the industrial engineering and work measurement function logically begins with a comprehensive analysis of time study procedures. One preferred method is to carefully study samplings taken at random from time study files. In a medium-sized department, 100 time studies might be considered representative; in a larger department, a greater number would be needed to develop adequate confidence in the results of the check. A time study supervisor, in looking at an individual study, may frequently note deficiencies here and there, but the deficiencies are seldom acted upon from the observation of a few isolated studies. The impact of large numbers of the same type of shortcoming as observed from a larger sampling permits the development of more objective evaluations. One recommended procedure is to make a spread sheet and then record comments from each study on the sheet as satisfactory or unsatisfactory against each of the following criteria:

1. Proper and complete entries of basic information: part number, operator, date of study, machine number, operation number, and so on. The time of beginning and ending of the study should be noted.

2. A complete description of the operation. It should be adequate enough to tell exactly what is being done, what motions are involved, and the exact methods and distances involved so that anyone generally familiar with the nature of the work being performed in the particular shop will be able to recognize the operation.

3. Proper designation of each element of the operation: separation of constant times from variable times, separation of machine times from manual times, left-hand and right-hand notations where applicable, notation of break points, and so on. If proper designation is not made, revision becomes difficult, particularly in view of the frequent clauses in union contracts that restrict changes resulting

from new methods to the elements affected. If the elements are not carefully defined, it is often impossible to substantiate such changes.

4. Complete notation of machine speeds, feeds, or similar equipment settings whenever they are applicable.

5. Proper notation and handling of foreign elements.

6. Mathematical accuracy.

7. Proper notation and application of performance levels.

8. Notation of all tools and special equipment.

9. Proper handling of allowances.

10. Adequate number of readings.

11. Sketch or photograph of operation or workplace layout where applicable.

12. General impression of neatness and arrangement of data and orderly development of the mathematics of the standard so that anyone who has not made the time study can follow through the mathematical procedures and verify them.

An example of a checklist corresponding to the preceding criteria is shown in Figure 18. The notations are from an actual survey.

Leveling

Data from the spread sheet, Figure 18, can be used to study the overall impact of leveling or performance rating. It is difficult for anyone not present at the time a study is taken to make any valid judgment of the accuracy of the leveling factor used. However, a distribution curve of a number of levelings as taken from a large number of time studies often gives an indication of the concept within the plant. If it is subdivided by groups of individual time study men, such a curve may provide a measure of the consistency of performance ratings between various individuals.

Ideally, the distribution should approximate a normal one with the midpoint at average, or 100 percent, and a general bell shape. Any radical departure suggests a further look at the skills of the time study staff in this important function. Often the distribution of leveling approximates the distribution of incentive gains, and there is good reason to believe that the relationship is sound unless distorted by other factors.

It has been found that time study men are hesitant to level performance below 100 percent, perhaps because of union pressure or a reluctance to antagonize individual operators. However, if we con-

Figure 18. Spread sheet for the evaluation of time studies.

Date _____

Plant _____

S — Satisfactory
0 — Not shown
X — Error
U — Unsatisfactory
NA — Not Applicable
HI — High
L — Low

Part No.	Operation No.	General Description of Operation	Element Breakdown and Description	Machine Setting, Speed, Feed, etc.	Foreign Elements	Mathematics	Leveling	Tooling Noted	Allowances*	No. of Readings	Sketch	Start & Finish Times	General Appearance	Base Time
53724	5	S	S	NA	O	X	115	S	6-5	HI	O	O	S	14.56
53628	10	S	S	NA	O	S	120	S	6-5	L	O	O	S	10.96
44872	5	S	U	NA	O	S	115	U	9-5	S	O	O	U	62.48
93574	15	S	S	S	U	U	120	S	8-5	L	O	S	U	12.37
88523	5	S	U	U	S	S	105	S	9-5	S	S	O	U	24.78
65490	10	S	S	NA	O	S	115	U	8-5	L	O	S	S	20.04
44489	20	U	S	NA	O	U	110	S	9-5	S	O	O	S	2.20
63998	30	S	S			S	115	S	8-5	L	O	O	U	12.18
43299	10	U	S				105	S	10-5			O		18.93
12367	5				U									
				NA	U									
			U	NA	U	U	115		6-5	L	O	O	S	10.30
	5	U	S	S	O	U	110	S	8-5	L	O	O	U	8.78
10346	10	U	U	NA	O	S	120	U	9-5	L	S	O	S	46.91
11145	5	S	U	NA	O	X	125	S	9-5	L	O	O	U	11.87
30711	5	U	S	NA	O	S	125	S	9-5	L	O	O	S	21.40
Summary:		17S 8U	19S 6U	19NA 4S 2U	130 12U	15S 7U 3X	Min. 105 Max. 125	18S 7U		13L 8S 4H	120 4S	5S 200	13S 12U	

*First figure shown is fatigue and delay allowance.
Second figure shown is standard personal allowance.

sider 100 percent as *average* performance within a plant, there should logically be as many people below the 100 percent level as there are above it.

For example, in an investigation involving a fabricator of large sheet-metal components, it was felt that the concept of leveling on the part of the time study staff was quite liberal. A representative sample of time studies showed that the average leveling factor was approximately 115 percent, and there were no ratings below 100 percent. In other words, the concept of average pace was too liberal by about 15 percent. That coincided with the actual level of incentive gains within the plant, which were about 15 percent above normal expected values. A series of rating sessions with the time study staff substantiated the suspicion that the staff concept of leveling was too liberal. The condition was subsequently improved by a number of additional training sessions and the use of a variety of training films.

Standard Data

One of the most important factors in evaluating the work of the standards department is the development and use of standard data. The ability of the department to develop an objective type of standard data separates superior from mediocre performance. An investigation of this function should include a study of the percent of rates that are set from standard data as compared with the percent set by conventional time study methods.

The quality of the standard data developed should be judged by the criteria given in the section on standard data in Chapter 3. Macrometric data so described have all the advantages of ready application with a minimum of clerical work, but, like conventional time studies, they should have substantiations of exact methods, that is, specific data on machine times, feeds and speeds, material handling, and consistency of break points, all of which are acknowledged as criteria of a competent individual time study. Without the reference material, standard data can become just as obsolete as individual time studies, since they are subject to the same technological and other changes.

Any evaluation of the industrial engineering function from the standpoint of the development of standard data should include investigation of how the standards group performs its own activities. Standard data should be audited frequently and carefully, particularly because standard data, by their very nature, are widely applied. Therefore, any obsolescence of or inaccuracy in the data is multiplied by the frequency of data use and can result in inaccurate incentives and distorted labor costs over large quantities or operations. Thus, the maintenance of standard data requires frequent and conscientious auditing.

Delay Allowances

The handling of the various delay allowances merits considerable study. Far too many standards departments still apply allowances to work standards in a haphazard manner. For example, requirements for personal time are generally well standardized at between 3 and 5 percent, but there is still a considerable tendency to group all fatigue and delay allowances at some nominal figure such as 15 percent, without reference to actual determination of what is included in the allowances or whether or not they are suited to the specific situation. Work sampling studies will frequently reveal a wide variation in the types of delays and necessary allowances encountered in different types of occupations within the same plant or even within the same work center. All these should be set up on some factual basis, and a detailed listing of the various types of delays should be included in the standard allowances. They also should be reviewed from time to time, since delay items are just as subject to change as the methods by which work is done.

Standard Practice Instruction

The proper development of incentives requires consistent techniques within the standards department and uniform procedures on the part of all individual time study men. Uniformity can be attained only by a written manual of standard practice. The manual should contain not only the company's standard policy on wage incentives (see Appendix A) but also detailed techniques to be used in the conduct and development of time studies. Specifically, the manual should include:

1. Procedures for filling out all necessary general information on the study: part name, part number, operator, machine, description of operation, and start and finish times of the study.

2. General instructions for element description and break points, as well as instructions for separating variables from constants and manual time from machine time.

3. Instructions on proper leveling procedures to be used, including policies on proper handling of subnormal or above-normal performance.

4. Details on the arithmetic of the system involved, including handling of allowances (fatigue, personal, delays, machine, incentive).

5. Procedures for handling machine- or process-controlled operations.

6. General policy concerning the use of group and individual incentives.

7. Procedures to be used where performance cannot be standardized, as in new work, repairs, and experimental work.

8. Instructions on methods of developing standard data.

9. Approvals required for time studies, as by foremen and chief of standards.

10. Proper clerical procedures for establishing the standard and furnishing the timekeeping department with proper information.

11. Temporary rates; procedures for establishing and canceling temporary rates when standard rates cannot be applied.

Manuals that include material of this type are necessary for consistent application of incentives. They are vitally needed not only because there is a possibility of union scrutiny of disputed standards but also to maintain consistent procedures in spite of changes in standards personnel.

Methods Engineering

The responsibility for proper manufacturing methods is one of the more common assignments to the industrial engineering or standards department. The effectiveness of the department in this respect is best determined by observing typical operations on a tour of the shop. Criteria for evaluation should be based on proper applications of the well-known principles of motion economy and work design. For example:

- Are tools, materials, bins, and racks properly arranged for easy access and disposal of finished parts?
- Are fixtures designed to eliminate or minimize problems of holding and locating parts? Is maximum use of combined tooling being made?
- Are methods designed to permit the most effective use of body members: the use of both hands, elimination of idle and waiting times, elimination of holding? Is the design of the workplace such that a maximum amount of work is performed in the normal area?*

We have mentioned previously that the full industrial engineering approach—methods improvement, measurement, and application of proper incentives—has resulted in improvements in productivity to

---

* For a checklist of 22 rules and principles of motion economy that can be profitably applied to shop and office work alike and is an excellent guide for an audit see Ralph M. Barnes, *Motion and Time Study: Design and Measurement of Work*, 6th Ed. (New York: John Wiley & Sons, Inc., 1968), p. 220.

about twice the levels obtainable through unplanned daywork performance. About half of those improvements are usually the result of developing and standardizing proper methods. Therefore, if the effectiveness of the industrial engineering department is being evaluated, one of the most important criteria is its contribution in the area of methods improvement.

A good procedure in performing an audit of methods improvement is to make a rough sampling based on informal observations of a representative number of operations and judge them by the criteria of good motion economy as satisfactory, acceptable, or unsatisfactory. The judgments should be based on how carefully the principles of motion economy have been applied to the particular operation and whether substantial improvement is still possible.

It is methods improvement that distinguishes the industrial engineer from the rate setter. However, the complete evaluation of the factor must also be related to factors external to the industrial engineering department, especially the degree to which senior management has been able to get shop supervision to recognize its own responsibilities in applying standard methods and in assisting industrial engineering with methods improvement. The job cannot be done by industrial engineers alone. If they are expected to develop improved methods, they must be given the necessary technical and organizational tools, including not only adequate staff but also the proper organizational climate.

8

The Shop Administration Factor

INCENTIVE STANDARDS based either on time study or on standard data represent a measured concept of performance under presumed standardized conditions. Such standards, whether they are used for rewarding increased output, measuring shop levels of performance, or planning for production schedules, represent a vitally necessary tool for manufacturing administration. The intelligent use of the tool is a responsibility of shop administration; it cannot be shifted back to the standards department. The very considerable potential gains of wage incentives can be either achieved or lost completely by shop supervision. The proper evaluation of that function thus becomes an important factor in measuring the effectiveness of the wage incentive plan.

Timekeeping and Methods Charges

Shop administration of the wage incentive plan comprises two major areas. The first is reporting or timekeeping. All work done must be properly accounted for by credits for work done on standard operations, credits for quantities produced, accurate accounting for time spent, and assurance that quality has been maintained.

The second factor covers the recognition by supervisors that all manufacturing is done in an atmosphere of continual change. Supervisors must completely accept their responsibility to see that all changes in methods, procedures, tooling, quality of incoming materials, and changes in delay factors are promptly recognized and reported for adjustment to the incentive structure.

No incentive plan can long survive severe shortcomings in either area of shop administration. Supervisory failure to accept responsibilities in these two areas will only hasten the demise of the wage incentive plan no matter how well the plan has been conceived or is administered at the industrial engineering level. The problem is so important that a consultant who is investigating any kind of wage incentive problem will almost invariably audit the administration of the plan at shop level.

The background for such an audit is the concept that, in a broad sense, manufacturing is a system where the inputs are materials, labor, tooling, and factory services. The outputs are usually products. The relation between the inputs and outputs determines operating efficiency. A wage incentive plan with its standards thus becomes an important factor in measuring inputs of labor on a quantitative basis. The approach can also be used to measure such supporting services as maintenance, material handling, and setups. The measured inputs can thus be used to relate performance in terms of physical output of product and in the necessary maintenance of the manufacturing facility: buildings, capital equipment, and tooling.

Any tinkering with the inputs, such as not reporting methods improvements or permitting excess charges against accounts such as material handling and lost time in order to maintain some socially desirable level of incentive earnings, merely disguises inefficient performance and adds to the input cost. An example of this was found in the shipping room of a large manufacturer of electric motors. An audit revealed that the shipping department foreman was arbitrarily adding a large number of hours to miscellaneous service accounts (material handling, for example) on the tally sheet in order to bring the incentive earnings of his department up to a desired level.

Another well-known tactic is to permit an operator who is setting up his machine on a daywork basis to produce a quantity of finished pieces before clocking in on the production run under an incentive plan. Any operations that involve a considerable amount of split time (change from daywork to incentive operations or vice versa) offers unlimited opportunities for enhancing incentive earnings by varying time clock punchings to indicate greater amounts of daywork than was performed and correspondingly smaller amounts of incentive time. Table 6 indicates how this may be done. Without adequate control, such practices permit the operators to virtually write their own payroll. That not only costs unnecessary labor dollars but also disguises any poor performance.

Excessive incentive earnings on loose rates are often banked, which means that complete production is not reported until some later date. There are numerous situations in which less than normal incentive gains are concealed by reporting nonexistent daywork. In an off-the-record conversation with a consultant, a union steward once said that he no longer discussed problems of inadequate rates with any of his foremen because a foreman would just respond with, "Don't you know how to use a red card [daywork allowance]?"

Where such a situation exists, what importance can be attached to performance and timekeeping records? The ordinary factory accounting procedure gives no indication of such reporting errors, and management is lulled into a sense of false security. The reasonable conclusion is that the incentive plan is functioning normally; the mal-

Table 6. Example of inflated earnings due to improper time reporting.

(Incorrectly reported times are underlined.)

Work Done	Actual Work Situation		Misrepresented Record	
	Working Hours	Hours Paid	Hours Reported	Hours Paid
Setup	7 A.M. to 9:45 A.M., daywork	2.75	7 A.M. to 10 A.M.	3.00
Operate	9:45 A.M. to 12 noon, incentive; produced 500 pieces at standard rate of 6.0 hours ÷ 100 Actual incentive gain: 3.0 standard hours ÷ 2.25 actual hours = 133 %	3.00	10 A.M., to 12 noon Same production. Reported incentive gain: 3.0 standard hours ÷ 2.00 actual hours = 150 %*	3.00
Tear down, make new setup	12:30 to 2:00 P.M., daywork	1.50	12:30 to 2:30 P.M., daywork	2.00
Operate	2:00 to 3:30 P.M. Produced 100 pieces at standard rate of 2.0 hours ÷ actual incentive gain: 2.0 standard hours ÷ 1.5 actual hours = 133 %	2.00	2:30 to 3:30 P.M. Same production. 2.00 standard hours ÷ 1.0 actual hour = 200 %*	2.00
	Total hours	9.25		10.00
	Cost at $3.00 per hour	$27.75		$30.00

Increase in average hourly earnings by incorrect reporting

$$\frac{\$30.00 - \$27.75}{8 \text{ hours}} = \frac{\$2.25}{8} = \$0.28 \text{ per hour}$$

* Note how this device can also be used to show fictitious incentive gains.

functions can be discovered only by an audit. A complete audit of the recording or timekeeping function must answer these questions:

- Are the start and completion of each job recorded *immediately?*
- Who enters rates on timekeeping records? Are preprinted operation tickets used? Are entries audited?
- Who counts output? Are counts audited? Can they be verified from other records?
- Who is responsible for quality?
- What is the policy on rework of defective material?
- What controls are in use for proper handling of special allowances for lost time and defective material?

Given a centralized timekeeping office, work sampling will often reveal whether employees are actually working on the jobs for which they are punched in. On the other hand, when employees retain their own labor tickets, auditing is more difficult and is then best performed on a random basis. An unannounced plant tour made shortly before the end of a shift frequently reveals symptoms of loose reporting. If a walk through the plant reveals an excessive number of idle employees, including some who are writing up their labor tickets, suspicion can be directed to timekeeping. Interviews with industrial engineering personnel and with the foremen will bring to light attitudes toward proper handling of timekeeping. At times, the auditor needs considerable skill to dig into the real situation.

The vital function in maintaining an incentive system is continuing correction of standards with changes in method. The attitude and motivation of the foreman in reporting methods changes and improvements to industrial engineering often reflect how well the foreman has been trained by top management. One good way to check this situation is to take a sampling of actual jobs being run in the plant at the time, record in detail the methods being used, and then refer to the time study files or operation sheets for verification of method.

Abuses of Reporting

The reporting of methods changes and improvements to the industrial engineering function for a recheck of the rates is extremely difficult to audit. Such changes and improvements come from a multitude of sources and occur in a variety of places. Some changes directly affect the operation and are immediately noticeable. Others, particularly in assembly operations, may occur gradually over long periods of time and arise from a variety of causes. The changes are extremely difficult to evaluate quantitatively.

Elaborate systems for reporting changes generally are unreliable. In the course of audit in a plant manufacturing electrical transformers, an extremely high proportion of operations were found to have been changed and improved from the methods recorded on the original time studies. In that plant, each foreman was required, each week, to report any changes made in methods or procedures in his department. A study of reports revealed that, for the preceding six months, one foreman had simply written "no change" on each weekly report and signed his name. Obviously, the problem was one of top management motivation rather than ineffective industrial engineering.

Foremen's Activities

In justice to the average foreman, the demands on his time and abilities are seldom recognized by top management. Most of the manufacturing problems related to personnel, production shortages, quality, failure to meet schedules, tooling, incentives, grievances, and proper methods usually wind up on his desk for proper solution or recommendation. Frequently, an informal work sampling of the foreman's daily activities will provide valuable information about the amount of time he has to spend on various problems. Proper use of the information may result in finding ways to improve his effectiveness by providing him with additional staff help, improving communications, or reorganizing his work to give him maximum time for the accomplishment of his main function, which is the supervision of his people and their activities. He cannot perform that important function if he is required to spend most of his time in chasing down stock, filling out reports, or attending endless meetings.

There is no reason why the industrial engineering or standards department cannot carry out a successful methods-and-systems study of the foreman's activities by using the principles that are applied in the design of productive operations. If such a study is carried out in a sympathetic and cooperative manner, it can do much to improve the relations between the standards people and the shop supervisors.

Many of the supervisory incentives applied to foremen are poorly designed. The most important of the foreman's many responsibilities include (1) producing a product of required quality, (2) maintaining required labor, materials, and overhead costs, and (3) meeting production schedules. Therefore, any supervisory incentive should be based on a measurement of all three functions. Also, it should be based not only on the performance of his own department but on plantwide operations as well. Any supervisory incentive that stresses only one of the three functions will merely result in excessive attention to that function and corresponding neglect of the others. (See Chapter 2 for a detailed analysis of factors to be considered in developing a supervisory incentive.) For example, a bonus related to incentive gains alone merely acts as a motivating factor toward keeping the incentive system as loose as possible. Often that puts the foreman on the side of the employees and invites warfare with the standards department.

Auditing
the Incentive System

A fact-finding audit of the administration of a wage incentive system in a small department is typical of one approach to a study of administration of wage incentives. The department was one of about eight employees in a machinery building plant in the midwest, and the work consisted of assembling subcomponents of larger pieces of equipment. Tolerances were exacting and quality requirements exceedingly close, which required a high order of employee skill.

The department was operating under individual incentives, but it had experienced a long period of unsatisfactory earnings that had been the subject of considerable company-union controversy. The company through its staff had consistently maintained that the rate structure was sound and that the low earnings were simply due to lack of effort; the union contended that operating delays within the department were largely responsible for the low earnings.

An audit was conducted by a combination of intensive work sampling and group time studies covering all the men working in the department. Observations were made at random intervals to obtain statistical accuracy in the work-delay pattern of the employees. Each operator was contacted at frequent intervals throughout each day to record the nature of his activities, and performance ratings of the individual employees were also made during the study. A total of 688 observations made over a period of 6 working days covered the activities of all seven employees. Thus, the study represented observations of 42 man-days of work. The audit permitted factual evaluation of the following:

- Adequacy and consistency of the rate structure as it was currently applied.
- Employee performance, with a consideration of both skill and effort.
- Nature and extent of any other factors that would affect performance.

By the study it was possible to develop a relationship between the skill and effort ratings of the individual employees and their earnings under incentive, discover inconsistencies in the incentive structure between components of similar work content, and reevaluate numerous delay factors affecting production. The categories used in classifying the observations were as follows:

Constructive work, manual
Constructive work, machine
Production delays
Delays in waiting for material or instructions
Time to change shift
Personal time
Fatigue
Idle time
Time to punch out
Operator not in the department
Miscellaneous delays

The summaries indicated that only 50 percent of available operator time was spent on constructive work and about 33 percent on delays beyond operator control. The department was probably typical of many manufacturing operations. The reasons for lack of good incentive performance were not confined to a single cause such as poor rates but resulted from a combination of numerous administrative effects, in addition to some discrepancies and inconsistencies in the rate structure. In the particular situation involved not only were the unavoidable delays at an excessive level but the auditor was able to record that very few jobs once started could be completed without some interruption due to part shortages or poor quality of a specific component. An important point that had previously gone unrecognized was that, because of problems in other areas, the foreman was able to spend only about a third of his time in the department.

Intensive work sampling or group time studies of an entire work center becomes an invaluable device in determining what is wrong with a wage incentive in a particular area. The study described here was completed with about six man-days of observation plus approximately five days for developing the data and writing the finished report, so that within two weeks the interested parties had a factual confirmation of the exact nature of the problems in the department.

In dealing with such problems, group studies have numerous advantages over conventional work sampling procedures. They produce

Figure 19. Form for audit of standards.

Part Number	Operation Number	Latest Issue	Information Complete	Correlation with Operations	Information Complete	Correlation with Routing	Proper Motions and Work Station	Correlation with Original Time Study	Element desc. and Breakdown	Time Standard – %	Timing	Allowances	Calculations	Approvals	Neatness	
1.																
2.																
3.																
4.																
5.																
6.																
7.																
8.																
9.																
10.																
Summary: S																
X																
% S																

Engineering Drawing · Routing · Time Study Correlation · Observed

Plant _____
Date _____
Audit by _____

Remarks & Notes

Remarks and Recommendations: _____

S — Satisfactory
X — Discrepancy or Unsatisfactory
N — Not required
O — Check not made

quite reliable results within a short period of time; they are much more analytical than conventional work sampling; and they permit a broader-based approach than lengthy individual studies.

The administrative audit of a wage incentive program differs from the time study audit, which is intended to evaluate how well the standards department follows good time study techniques. However, in this chapter we are discussing shop adherence to established standards and such an administrative audit follows a different approach. It is intended primarily to audit the nature and extent of changes that may have occurred in the shop subsequent to the original time study or standard data application and point out areas in which there is a need to either tighten up shop proceedings or establish a regular scheduled audit program.

Example of an Audit

One method of recording observations and data for an administrative audit of wage incentives is illustrated in Figure 19. The following is a procedural instruction for such an audit. On the occasion of its use the audits were performed at branch factory locations by an industrial engineer from corporate headquarters.

TIME STANDARDS AUDIT PROCEDURE

This audit is intended to give a sampling of compliance with recognized and necessary procedures on good wage incentive administration. It is intended to point out areas where improvement is required in shop administration, compliance with standardized methods, and the degree to which shop supervision notifies the Standards Department regarding methods changes. It is not intended that observed discrepancies be corrected by the person making the audit; such corrections are a function of Plant Industrial Engineering and Plant Management. Audits should be made in collaboration with the Plant Industrial Engineer, and all findings are to be reviewed with him as well as the Plant Manager. Where an unusually large proportion of discrepancies are noted, it is intended that a second audit will be made after a short period.

The auditor will check shop schedules and select at random orders that are being run in each supervisor's area.

He will then obtain the latest drawing and route sheet for each item as well as time studies and operation analysis sheets for selected operations on each route sheet. The detailed audit program follows:

Audit as follows:
1. Check each drawing for:
    A. Latest issue used.
    B. Adequacy of information.
2. Check routings for:
    A. Correct operations.
    B. Proper description.
3. Check time studies for:
    A. Correlation with routing data.
    B. Proper work station and motion pattern.
    C. Adequate methods record.
    D. Proper timing.
    E. Proper allowances.
    F. Correct calculations.
    G. Proper approvals.
    H. Neat and orderly arrangement.
4. Check operation analysis for:
    A. Agreement with time study.
    B. Complete information.
5. Check actual shop run for:
    A. Correlation of actual method with operation analysis.
    B. Compare time standard as observed with actual standard.
6. Check foreman for:
    Agreement with and understanding of time study.
7. Check timekeeper for:
    Agreement between posted and correct standard.

This audit was directed primarily to administrative areas—use of proper drawings and routings and the correlation of time studies with actual conditions observed in the shop. It was not heavily directed toward evaluation of time study techniques as such, except for general notations concerning correct procedures and agreement with shop conditions, unlike the audit procedures described in Chapter 7 as a check on the competence of the standards department.

9

Plan Maintenance

THE EVALUATIONS described in Chapters 6 to 8 will reveal strengths and weaknesses in the operation of the wage incentive plan and should indicate areas in which improvements are needed. The analyses will also provide a basis for maintenance designed to keep the incentive plan operating at maximum effectiveness and prevent its deterioration through obsolescence. Maintenance programs are relatively new; most plans and procedures for auditing and maintenance of wage incentives were developed during the sixties.

Maintenance programs for incentives should follow the basic principles of preventive maintenance programs for mechanical equipment, namely, continual checking and adjusting of minor problems before they become serious and cause equipment shutdowns. However, very few managers today recognize the need for that function. They will unhesitatingly call in outside accountants to check inventories, accounts receivable, and other financial figures, but fail completely to recognize that a function that directs the expenditures of a large part of their direct labor needs the same type of auditing and maintenance. To a considerable degree, this can be construed as objective criticism of the industrial engineering profession, which has in the past concerned itself largely with the measurement function and spent much educational effort and engineering development toward greater and greater accuracy in the measurement of productive operations. It has not shown a corresponding concern for what happens to the measurements once made, nor has it sufficiently emphasized the importance of maintenance to its own management.

It is a fairly common experience of those who discuss a wage incentive situation with top management to be told that the incentive system was installed many years before by a very reputable consulting firm that must have done a good job because there had been no trouble with the system for years. Yet the briefest and most casual check of operating conditions frequently reveals that the lauded plan is hopelessly out of date.

This chapter, therefore, will emphasize preventive maintenance techniques. The first part of the chapter will deal with techniques for maintaining the consistency of the standards with methods in use in the shop.

Auditing of Standards

One method for consistent auditing of new standards that has been used in a number of plants is to fill out a card when the new standard is issued. The card shows the part number, operation, and number of the new standard and also a date when the standard is to be reviewed. The card is then filed by review date and, when brought up by the standards clerk, forms the basis for an auditing schedule.

Timing of the reviews should be based on the relative importance and frequency of the operation. Work that is done frequently and that represents a considerable investment in labor dollars can be audited as often as every two or three months; operations that are performed less often can be reviewed at intervals of six months or a year. Basically, the plan provides for a systematic review of every incentive rate. It is generally considered good practice to assign the most competent members of the standards department to the review function. The same approach should be used in reviewing standard data, since they also are subject to continuing obsolescence.

A variation of the card method, when rates are applied at shop level, is to rubber-stamp the rate file whenever a rate is to be audited with "Do not apply rate, call Standards for audit." The timekeeper then notifies the person in charge of the audit function that the job or operation in question is starting in the shop.

An approach that is well adapted to smaller plants is to systematically review all the rates in a given work center or department at one time and then proceed to the next department or work center.

After the entire plant has been covered by the procedure, the cycle is repeated.

Because auditing and maintenance of wage incentive plans is a relatively new development, there is no well-defined pattern of auditing. However, the increasing recognition of the importance of the function is borne out by a survey conducted by the Milwaukee Chapter of the Society for the Advancement of Management. Replies to the question, "Do you have a definite program for auditing standards?" revealed that, of 34 companies reporting, 21 had such a program and 13 had not. Other responses indicated that a large proportion of the companies were unionized. Thus, it seems reasonable to assume that such an auditing program can be carried out in a unionized plant as well as in a non-unionized one. Informally, some union officials indicate that there could be agreement on a formalized audit program if it were kept completely factual and applied systematically.

CHANGES

Audits usually will reveal numerous deviations from prior practice; they will come under the headings of (1) unreported methods changes, (2) changes in operations due to more uniform and consistent quality of components, (3) operator-instituted improvements, and (4) creeping changes.

Unreported methods changes. Definite methods changes are usually the simplest to effect because adjustment is based on known conditions and well-defined changes. They are usually made as a result of new tools or fixtures or as the result of design changes in the part that alter the amount of work necessary. These changes are frequently but not always reported under existing maintenance of rate programs. However, in this situation timing is important. Although the change may be easy to document, revising a standard because of a methods change is not always easy. A recent change will be well remembered and can be documented; a change that has gone unreported for a long period of time is more difficult to justify. After a certain period of time it can be argued that the company has acquiesced in not altering the standard.

Changes in operations due to more uniform and consistent quality of components. Changes that are due to improvement in component quality are more difficult to measure and evaluate than planned changes. They could be changes either in the incoming quality of purchased parts or parts to be assembled or in modifications in quality requirements within the operation itself. For example, improved foundry practices generally create substantial reductions of time needed for preparing castings for final use, such as cleaning and filing burrs, and often reductions in machining time as well. Similarly, improvements in control of tolerances of assembly components may effect substantial savings in assembly time. They tend to reduce the time required for fitting, filing, shimming, and adjusting. In such a situation, much depends on how well the original standards were documented.

Operator-instituted improvements. Here the operator through experience or ingenuity has developed a better method of performing the operation, often with the aid of simple mechanical devices. Management must recognize that employees who are working on a specific operation for long periods of time are frequently in a position to make important contributions to methods improvement. The process is a continuing one, and there is hardly an incentive installation in existence that has not experienced numerous instances of minor or even major improvements in operations as a result of operator ingenuity.

This type of change is seldom reported, and in many situations it is tacitly considered to be the operator's personal privilege and property. That philosophy might be tolerable if there were some assurance that the operator who developed the new method would be the only one to benefit from its use. However, with the usual transfers and personnel changes, new methods generally become common property and their benefits accrue to individuals who had nothing to do with the improvement. The net result then is a frozen rate and more inconsistency in the incentive structure. The predominant policy in any wage incentive administration must be that the standard reflects the method in use. Rigid adherence to that principle requires that the standard be immediately studied and revised.

By itself the net effect of that procedure would be to create a disgruntled operator and completely stifle improvements in methods by employees. Proper handling requires rewarding the operator for his contribution and encouraging others to imitate him. The preferred method is to reward the operator with a sum of money commensurate with his contribution, after the basic principles and methods of a suggestion system. Since the payment is one-time, it can be quite liberal. The company is then morally free to immediately restudy the method and apply the revised standard. It will then benefit from the savings due to the improved method and preserve the integrity of the rate structure. Furthermore, the procedure will encourage similar improvements from other employees.

One large company that has a well-planned audit system permits an employee who has developed a new method for his operation the following choices: He may report the improvement immediately. In this option, the employee is given a bonus based on the value of his contribution and the rate is changed immediately. Or he may continue to benefit from the increased earnings accruing under the improved method until the operation is audited. At that time the incentive rate will be corrected on the basis of the new study.

Creeping changes. Creeping changes are probably the most difficult type of adjustment to handle. The accumulation of many minor changes, often of such a minute nature as to be difficult to measure, may loosen up an entire rate structure. The changes might include improved material handling and better delivery of supplies or improved tool life as a result of either improved tool steel or better cutting compounds.

The evaluation of creeping changes, if they are noted, should be as factual as possible so that the improvements can be specifically and quantitatively related to conditions existing at the time of the original study. The conditions are frequently observed where it is difficult to differentiate between many minor changes. Sometimes it is possible to record minor changes and change the rate when the changes have accumulated to some fixed percentage, frequently 5 percent.

IDENTIFYING THE KIND OF CHANGE

It is frequently difficult to distinguish between improvements in incoming parts, improvements in operator skills, and creeping changes. In this area much depends on the judgment and shop knowledge of the standards people and the completeness of the original time study data. For example, an intricate locating motion that is used to place a part in a fixture may initially require two or three separate alignment stops. As a result of experience gained over thousands of repetitions, the skilled operator may become so automatic and so rhythmic that the individual locating points become almost imperceptible.

Another case might involve the assembly operation of a gearbox. The average operator might require two or three trial adjustments with varying thicknesses of shims before he attains the proper match of gears; the skilled operator may be able to judge existing clearances by feel and, in practically all cases, select the proper shims at the first try. Such improvements are not so much changes in method as they are acquired skills. A thorough background of shop knowledge and practice is required as a background for audits of such operations.

Proper treatment of the factor skills implies recognition of the learning curve (the progress function). Use of the learning curve can be very helpful when there is pressure to apply incentives to new work before an operator is fully trained. When good data are available, new operations can be put on incentive before the operators are fully trained. As discussed in Chapter 3, the use of training allowances creates maximum motivation for the learner.

Order quantities affect learning and are a significant factor related to the development of operator skills. In the average shop, new models or new products generally start their productive life in relatively small quantities. In that period, the standards department is under the greatest pressure to apply incentives to the new work. Every pressure is used—first to increase production and then to decrease cost. If the model or product becomes successful, repeat orders will be based on larger and larger production quantities.

During the growth period, the major obsolescence of the incentives takes place as a result of the introduction of improved tooling, better methods, and improved operator skills. For that reason, changes in lot size should be included as justifiable reasons for changes in rates, but few if any union contracts embody changes in lot size, except for the general clause of job conditions, as reasons for adjusting rates. It is certainly apparent to most industrial engineers that such changes constitute legitimate justification for a restudy.

In other cases, changes in lot sizes may work in reverse. As a product goes through its life cycle and begins to approach the end of its popularity, lot sizes decrease, sometimes sharply. In such a case, methods and procedures that were economical for large runs are no longer applicable. Restudies may indicate upward adjustment of some rates.

Auditing of Timekeeping

Thus far our discussion has been directed toward maintaining the accuracy of standards and their proper relationship to the nature of the work being performed. Actually, this type of maintenance auditing covers only one phase of the activities of administering wage incentives. The other significant phase is the reporting or timekeeping function. Abuse of that function can be more costly and ruinous to the wage incentive system than the effect of a moderate number of inaccurate standards. Therefore, timekeeping audits should be just as carefully planned and programmed as audit of incentives.

In most industrial situations, the timekeeping and payroll functions are part of the responsibility of the accounting department, and for a number of reasons it is preferable to assign the timekeeping audits to representatives of the accounting staff. First, the accounting function is responsive to auditing techniques; auditing is a normal part of the training of the accountant. The function thus becomes a part of the internal audit and relieves the standards department of a duty that is somewhat outside of its normal range of activity. However, the planning of the audit should be a collaboration of the accounting and standards departments. The standards people, with their knowledge of shop administration, may be very helpful in directing the accounting effort to areas that are suspicious or in which incentive earning patterns indicate a malfunction in the system. Audits of timekeeping should consist of unannounced spot checks and should include the following:

- Random check of time cards to verify operator activity on specific jobs as indicated by the report.
- A sampling of records to insure that punch-outs for various lost time functions are factual and correct.
- Verification of piece count.
- Checks for proper application of specific rates and verification of operations and part numbers.
- A sampling of entries on records to determine that authorized rates are used.
- Checks for proper charging of work done on repairs and rework.

Such an audit must be completely random and unannounced. Its value stems from the disciplinary effect created by the knowledge that time cards and shop records are being checked. As in many other activities, the accuracy of the reporting function is maintained only by continuous surveillance.

Value of the Audit

The value of any audit lies only in the amount of corrective action initiated. An audit can only point out operating deficiencies and indicate areas in which corrective action is necessary. The proper support of each associated activity relative to maintenance of the incentive system is the responsibility of top management. The initiation of corrective action is a primary function of the line management and must begin with the top officer responsible for the manufacturing function—vice-president of manufacturing, factory manager, or whatever his title may be. If that person, in responsible charge of manufacturing, does not immediately and vigorously see to it that proper corrective action is taken on any shortcomings indicated by the audit, then the maintenance activity loses all its value and has the negative effect of undermining the attitudes of the staff departments responsible for creating and maintaining the incentive plan.

Table 7. Existing versus audited rates.

Part Number	Operation Number	Existing Rate, Hours per 100 Pieces	Rate Derived From Audit Study
4154	30	1.17	.95
4720	30	.80	.63
8654	35	.92	.62
4631	30	.88	.72
4745	40	.92	.65
6059	30	.95	.53
6608	35	.85	.43

The audit study of Table 7 is an example of the possible consequences of the lack of a planned program for maintenance of incentive rates. The data are from a series of independent time studies made for a Wisconsin manufacturer as part of an answer to a union grievance alleging tight rates. In this particular case, the existing rates were set from standards that had been developed four years previously and had not been audited or maintained. The audit study showed a variety of methods used by different operators on similar operations. Note that in spite of much use of standard data, existing rates were loose by an average of 43 percent for the seven operations audited. The sampling gives rise to the very interesting speculation: If the rates being grieved were 43 percent loose, how far out of line were the rates not being grieved?

10

Restrictive Factors
in Plan Operation

Behind most of the clauses in union contracts that relate to incentive systems are two opposing purposes. The purpose of the union is to preserve at all costs any gains or favorable conditions that may have accrued to its people regardless of how they were acquired. The purpose of the company is to keep itself competitive as a simple matter of survival not only for its own sake but for its employees' as well.

Many of the contract clauses that have been worked into union agreements as a result of union pressure are hedged with restrictive clauses that prevent flexible and efficient operation of the incentive plan. Management has often agreed to such clauses without attempting to foresee the effect on long-term labor costs and productivity.

UNION POLICY ON INCENTIVES

The most powerful factor in dealing with any union is precedent. Once a precedent has become well established as the way of doing things, the chances are that it will be extremely difficult to change. Typical precedents that are basic to union bargaining are that rates will not be tightened and that new methods are the only justification for rate changes.

The question that has become a major point in industrial relations is this: Are factors that freeze standards and perpetuate obsolete rates really fair in the long run? Are they fair to the workers either individually or collectively, to the customers, who might get a price reduction, or to the company, which might benefit from lower costs? The question really answers itself: Rates should never be frozen regardless of future changes. Errors, of whatever kind, should never be perpetuated.

Wage incentive clauses in union contracts can generally be grouped into three categories:

1. Attempts to control detailed techniques of the incentive plan. They include stipulations of the exact plan to be used, the nature of the time studies, the use of standard data or predetermined time, and plantwide allowance procedures.

2. Attempts to maintain incentive earnings under nonstandard conditions. They include restrictions on temporary rates, requirements that average earnings be paid for non-incentive work, and restrictions on the computation periods for rates.

3. Attempts to restrict rate revisions.

Attempts to Control Detailed Techniques

Most union contracts will specify the incentive plan to be used in the plant; it is usually based on the plan in use for productive workers. The following is a typical union clause:

> Incentive System. It is agreed that a "standard hour" incentive system will be maintained on the basis of actual time studies, standard data or estimated rates in cases where it is impractical to set a rate by actual time study or standard data. . . . The work required on the various operations will be measured by the time standards, which will be expressed in terms of standard hours per quantity of production of acceptable quality consistent with reasonable capacity of normal operators.

A clause of this type restricts the flexibility of the incentive plan and would make it impossible under the contract to extend incentive coverage to areas that involve unstructured or indirect operations for which a standard-hour plan might not be practical. The preferable substitute clause might read as follows:

Incentives may be applied to hourly work wherever the following conditions exist:

1. Where the work being done is measurable by recognized industrial engineering techniques.

2. Where there are available means for proper reporting of work completed and times actually spent.

3. Where the application of incentives would be of benefit to both the operator and to the company.

4. Where the cost of administering the particular incentive will not exceed the benefits to be derived from the application of the incentive.

Other clauses frequently restrict the type of standards development to recognized stopwatch time study practices that may not be applicable in all situations. The following is representative; comments are enclosed in brackets:

Time Study Policy

1. The steward of the department shall be notified prior to the beginning of any time study. Only workers normally working on the job may be time studied. [What happens when regular workers are not available or someone else is temporarily assigned? Does this paragraph mean that no studies may be made?]

2. The time study man shall record all of the conditions surrounding the job and shall record on the standard observation sheet: (a) A descriptive elemental breakdown of the operations, noting the sequence and outlining the method of performance. (b) A description of the condition of the material being worked on at the time of the time study, noting deviations from normal conditions, such as oily or greasy parts, excess stock, burrs, misfit parts, etc. [There is no indication of how these deviations are to be handled. Are they to be included in the permanent rate or are they to be made the subject of a separate allowance?]

3. All time studies shall be taken by the continuous watch reading method. [This is not always practical. Although continuous watch readings are desirable in most situations, there are many instances of work such that the exact sequence of operations does not repeat consistently. Continuous readings then become excessively cumbersome to handle.]

4. Whenever possible, operations shall be broken down into elements which will have clear break-off points.

5. When an operation is being studied, the number of pieces to be observed shall be of a sufficient number, or the duration of the study shall be extended, to be representative of actual conditions. [These are areas for the trained judgment of the time study man rather than the grievance procedures. The clause also invites futile haggling over inconsequential details.]

6. No watch reading shall be struck out in the taking of a time study unless a clear explanation of the reason therefor appears on the observation sheet. [This apparently harmless clause develops from the union's desire to protect its members from unethical practices or deliberate cheating on the part of the time study man. Actually, these demands usually arise from unresolved management problems. We must remember that the time study man has been given the responsibility for developing a standard in which the time allowances are based on proper methods and normal performance. He should not be expected to include in his standards such items as unnecessary delays, deliberate efforts to use time-consuming work procedures on the part of an operator who is attempting to get a liberal standard, or excessive attention to quality beyond that required by the nature of the work, nor should the standard include time consumed by improper tooling or improper quality of the material on which the operator is working. Such conditions, when they appear in a study, should not be included in the standard to be developed. When they are observed, they should be corrected by line supervision before the standard is applied. Frequently, lack of communication between the time study man and the foreman, lack of follow-up by the foreman, or lack of clear agreement on standards of quality may result in elements of work, delays, or time occasioned by improper methods being disallowed in the standard without the compensating correction of those conditions on the shop floor. Thus the union demand that addresses itself to the technique of time study is actually the result of inadequate shop practice or administration. The correction of the situation is the responsibility of line manufacturing supervision rather than that of the standards department staff.]

7. The observed time of each element, group of elements, or complete operation shall be leveled by the time study man.

8. One hundred (100) percent shall be considered normal. . . . The leveled time shall reflect the performance of the average worker, working efficiently at a job he can do well, working at

normal effort under the prescribed methods to produce the production standard (yield) under the conditions.

9. All production standards shall contain an allowance for personal time and for miscellaneous and minor delays. (a) Production standards for operations requiring manual clocking shall contain an allowance of not less than five (5) minutes per hour. [Time lost by punching a time clock (normally done between jobs) will vary according to the length of a job or assignment. For example, if a man worked all day on a job, the allowance specified here would donate a ridiculous total of 40 minutes for punching his time clock at the beginning and end of his shift.] (b) Production standards for operations which record all downtime by means of an electric clock inserted in the motivating electrical circuits, shall have an allowance of ten (10) percent added to the normal time. [From this we could infer that manual recording of downtime permits the operator to enhance his earnings by about 10 percent.]

Most of these procedures indicate standard industrial engineering practice for time study procedures for repetitive operations. However, many are not applicable where elements of work are not well developed or where there may be a wide variation of methods on the job. Paragraph 5, which calls for the number of pieces to be observed to be of a sufficient number, may frequently be impractical in that the run may be too short to be representative of average conditions. The allowances outlined in paragraph 9 represent an attempt to apply plantwide negotiated averages. In nearly all cases it is much better to base allowances on a study of each individual job and the nature of the delays inherent in that job. Table 8 indicates a more reasonable approach to the subject of fatigue allowances and also points up the variation in allowance with the type of work done.

RESTRICTIONS ON USE OF STANDARD DATA

Another very significant point is that all of these detailed procedures are based on the time study–rate setting ritual. There is almost no reference to the use, application, or development of standard data; in fact, much existing contract wording would preclude it. That position ignores the outstanding advantages of standard data that are discussed in Chapter 3. Whenever the wage incentive section of a union contract specifies time study methods in considerable detail, the clauses should include a statement that, when it is possible, rates will be set from standard data and that, when it is not possible,

Table 8. Fatigue allowances.

Type of Job	Tool Allow- ance*	Un- avoid- able Delay	Personal and Wash-up	Fatigue	Total Minutes	Percent†
Assembler, bench	0	10	25	11	46	10.6
Assembler, floor fixture	0	10	25	12	47	10.9
Brake, power—setup	0	20	25	11	56	13.2
Brake, power—operator	10	15	25	13	63	15.1
Deburr, bench	0	10	25	11	46	10.6
Drill press—setup	0	20	25	11	56	13.2
Drill press—operator	9	15	25	11	60	14.3
Drill press and router—setup	0	20	25	12	57	13.5
Drill press and router—operator	15	15	25	12	67	16.2
Drill, radial—setup	0	20	25	11	56	13.2
Drill, radial—operator	9	15	25	11	60	14.3
Former and finisher, metal—small	10	10	25	11	56	13.2
Former and finisher, metal—large	10	10	25	11	56	13.2
Form—roll and slitter—operator	10	15	25	11	61	14.6
Form—roll and slitter—tender	10	15	25	11	61	14.6
Grinding—Blanchard	4	15	25	11	55	12.9
Grinding—Ex-cello thread	15	15	25	11	66	16.0
Grinding—external	12	15	25	11	63	15.1
Grinding—internal	12	15	25	11	63	15.1
Lathe, engine	10	15	25	11	61	14.6
Lathe, turret—setup	0	20	25	11	56	13.2
Lathe, turret—operator	15	15	25	11	66	16.0
Mill—setup	0	20	25	11	56	13.2
Mill—operator	12	15	25	11	63	15.1
Mill—spar	15	15	25	11	66	16.0
Paint, spray	5	35	25	14	79	19.7
Press, hydraulic	5	15	25	12	57	13.5
Press, punch—setup	0	20	25	14	59	14.0
Press, punch—operator	0	15	25	14	54	12.7
Press, straightening	10	15	25	11	61	14.6
Rigger	0	10	25	13	48	11.1
Roll—setup	0	30	25	11	66	16.0
Roll—operator	5	15	25	11	56	13.2
Saw, Do-All—operator	10	15	25	11	61	14.6
Shear, rotary—light	5	15	25	13	58	13.7
Shear, rotary—heavy	10	15	25	15	65	15.7
Shear, square	10	15	25	15	65	15.7
Spinner, sheet metal	10	15	25	17	67	16.2
Stamp parts, bench	0	10	25	11	46	10.6
Swaging, machine—operator	10	15	25	11	61	14.6
Tube bender	0	10	25	11	46	10.6
Welder, spot—machine	15	10	25	14	64	15.4
Welder, spot—gun	15	10	25	15	65	15.7

* This allowance is calculated on the basis of all-day delay and tool-life studies.

† Method of computation: $\dfrac{\text{total minutes}}{\text{480 minutes (per workday)}} \times 100 = \text{percent}$

This table is reproduced by courtesy of E. A. Cyrol & Company, Chicago, Illinois.

individual time studies will be used in determining rates. The contract should also stipulate that it is the intent of the company to develop standard data on as much of the work being done as is practicable.

LEGITIMATE UNION INTERESTS

Actually, the stipulation of exact and detailed procedures to be used in taking time studies has no place in a union contract. The selection of time study procedures is a matter for professional judgment; appropriateness varies with the conditions. Nor is work measurement itself a simple clerical function; it is at least a technical and often a professional one. Competence in work measurement cannot be assured by establishing strict procedures; in fact, that course might preclude competence by putting strict limits on the work measurement function. As wage incentives are extended into indirect operations or into work that requires a high averaging of process variables, the simple time study procedures cease to be adequate and the newer techniques of work sampling, group time studies, and multivariant analyses are often required. Yet they would be prohibited by the usual contract.

Certainly the union has a legitimate interest in incentive standards, but its interest lies specifically in two areas: (1) Is a particular standard capable of producing median incentive earnings and is it consistent with existing standards for comparable or similar work? (2) Are the data used in developing the standard subject to factual verification? Beyond that, the selection of work measurement techniques should be reserved to management. A successful incentive system results from intelligent administration on the part of both the standards people and the shop supervisors rather than from narrow attention to specific details of the measurement function.

CONSEQUENCES OF RESTRICTIVE CLAUSES

It is significant that, once the specific clauses relating to time study procedures have been included in the contract and the contract is in effect, very little attention is paid to the clauses thereafter. The standards department goes about work measurement in its accustomed way, be it good, bad, or indifferent. In one observed situation the time studies in the files could only be considered as unacceptable. Operation and elemental descriptions were vague. Pertinent information on machine speeds and feeds and other similar information was frequently lacking. Elemental breakdowns were inadequate. Overall times were used instead of elemental analyses. The time studies were frequently illegible. All this was found in a plant where the union contract stipulated exact time study procedures.

Many contracts require that the time study man notify the operator of the pace at which he was leveled and the time for the operation before leaving. That effectively predicts the new standard without opportunity to verify the correctness of the method or the capability of the operator beyond immediate observation by the time study man. The leveling factor used then becomes a personal issue between the time study man and the operator.

Leveling factors should be discussed with the foreman, since the maintenance of proper employee performance is a function of the foreman and not the time study man. Nor can the time study man verify the consistency of the observed times with those in effect for other operations of similar work content. Good time study practice requires considerable analysis of the observed readings before the standard is developed, whereas the contract stipulation, in effect, requires that the standard be determined instantaneously. It also precludes standard data or statistical analyses.

The general effect of the objectionable procedures and limitations is heads I win, tails you lose: The company is committed to new rates without the thorough analysis needed to establish consistency with similar jobs, the union, on the other hand, can grieve any rates it considers unsatisfactory. Standards that are loose can immediately be accepted and become part of the established rate structure, and so the obsolescence of the incentive plan is hastened by continual loosening of rates.

Attempts to Maintain Unmerited Incentive Earnings

Here again we have two opposing policies. Union policy is that earnings must never be reduced regardless of how they have been derived; industrial engineering policy is that increased earnings above day rate shall accrue only because of effort and productivity above normal. Any attempt to apply incentive earnings to non-incentive conditions only dilutes the incentive plan and ultimately hastens its obsolescence. Typical of average earnings clauses are the following three. Comments are enclosed in brackets.

If a man because of his capabilities is removed from one piecework job and loaned or assigned to another department and not in accordance with seniority and is assigned to another piecework or daywork job, he shall be paid the average of the job from which he has been removed.

If a man is removed from a piecework job and loaned to another department and assigned to a daywork job, he shall be paid the average of the piecework earnings of the job he was removed from for that day only.

Incentive employees will be paid 25 percent above the direct rate for all nonstandard time except rework caused by the operator and normal cleanup. [This in effect guarantees that incentive employees will be paid at least 25 percent above day rate for any non-incentive work performed regardless of its nature.]

Provisions such as these not only dilute the incentive plan but also establish a precedent of paying incentive wages for non-incentive work. They frequently result in payment of various rates for the same type of work: Past earnings on one job or occupation are applied to another job or occupation.

There are many situations in which it is desirable to assign skilled employees to special types of work, such as research and development, in which their particular abilities are an asset. Inevitably the objection is raised that these employees are being penalized for their skill by loss of incentive earnings. In such cases it may be desirable to develop a special temporary wage based on some proportion of previous earnings, perhaps 85 percent, or to pay a flat allowance over and above the day rate. Either arrangement should be kept to a minimum and should be allowed only on approval by either the standards department or upper levels of manufacturing management. Approval at the foreman level usually results in loss of control.

Occasionally a union contract will become so loaded with restrictive clauses on incentives that some of the clauses are self-contradictory. For example, one contract outlines specifically the exact method to be used in time study, including the stipulation that no time study man shall leave a job he has studied before he informs the operator of the time required to perform the job or operation. After stipulating exact stopwatch procedures to be used and indicating the exact amount of personal fatigue, and unavoidable delay allowances to be used on a plantwide basis (regardless of the individual requirements of the operation), the contract further requires that the timing of any job will be averaged over the number of pieces run on any particular time study. That, of course would require the time study man to include any nonstandard deviations that occur in the course of his study. In the same contract is the clause:

> Standard time rates shall be set by the company so that an average competent incentive employee putting forth average effort based on normal production can earn no less than 25 percent above the direct rate as set forth in Schedule A attached hereto.

Since the "average, competent, incentive employee putting forth average effort" is impossible to define in specific terms, the natural result of this clause directs almost every earning situation below 25 percent to the grievance procedure regardless of cause.

STIPULATION OF MEDIAN GAINS

There are differences of opinion regarding the advisability of stipulating median incentive gains such as 25 percent in a union contract clause. It is true that with such a clause any new rate yielding less than the stipulated median earnings immediately becomes suspect. It is also true that in the absence of such a clause the union will immediately relate incentive gains on new rates or operations to the earnings produced by the loosest incentive rates that it can logically use for comparison. That will invite increased difficulties in the grievance procedure and certainly accelerate the deterioration of the incentive plan, since the tendency will be to relate all new rates to the earnings produced by older, established, and presumably looser rates. For that reason, the author feels that it is desirable to have the union contract specify the median incentive gains that the system is expected to produce. The governing clause might read as follows:

> New incentive rates will be set so that the average competent employee working at incentive pace will earn 25 percent above his base wage. However, failure to achieve such earnings shall not in itself indicate that the rate is incorrect.

A later clause in the contract under discussion reads as follows:

> Whenever jobs or operations are retimed . . . , the rate established by said retiming will be set so that hourly earnings will not be less than hourly earnings before such retiming provided the same amount of effort is applied.

The specified procedure would tend to perpetuate any looseness in existing rates that might have been caused by unreported methods changes and would require the same degree of looseness of the adjusted rate. Under this clause, the unfortunate time study man must not only follow an exactly prescribed procedure in developing his time study but also almost instantly inform the operator of the time allowance. Also, by some means or other, he must assure himself that he is in agreement with the stipulation that the average operator can earn no less than 25 percent above the direct rate or, in the case of rate revision, that the same level of incentive gains will be maintained as existed prior to the rate change. By agreeing to the clauses contained in the contract cited, management created an impossibly chaotic situation for its time study group, which is called upon to set rates that are consistent throughout the range of work being done and also, presumably, to assure the company that it will be getting optimum productivity for its labor dollar.

RATE ADJUSTMENTS

In another union contract are the clauses:

1. It is agreed that no existing incentive rates will be reduced.

2. It is agreed that in the event any present rates are deemed unfair, such rates will be adjusted so that incentive workers can earn a reasonable gain by working at an incentive pace. All new rates will be set in line with existing rates so as to produce earnings substantially equal to existing rates after the job is fully developed.

Note that the first clause flatly states that no rates are to be reduced. Strict application of the clause would be in complete disagreement with the accepted industrial engineering principle that the method on the job determines the time. According to the clause, all existing rates would be permanently frozen regardless of changes or improvements in tooling or methods.

The second clause of the contract fails to stipulate any policy as to what is expected as reasonable incentive gains. Also, it is ambiguous in that it specifies that new rates are to be set in line with existing rates but fails to define what existing rates are applicable to such an adjustment. Since the contract is silent about what are to be considered normal incentive gains, it can be expected that the union will demand a comparison with the highest possible earnings in a department or work center. A trend toward comparison with maximum incentive gains for all new rates can only hasten the obsolescence of the wage incentive plan. Also, setting new rates in line with earnings obtained by existing rates completely disregards the learning factor or changes of one type or another that may have loosened whatever existing rates are chosen for comparison.

SERVICE EMPLOYEES

Another procedure that is certain to become troublesome is to pay a service employee the average incentive earnings of the group he is servicing. There is then no measurement of his activities. Frequently he may be occupied for only a small portion of his time, and his actual workload may vary with changes in production schedules. A preferred method would be to measure his activities in terms of unit production, say, the assembly line he services, and then establish a separate material handling rate or include the work, as well as his input of time, in the final assembly rate. Management would then have some measure of control over the input of actual time.

STANDARDS FOR NEW WORK

Many union contracts stipulate that standards for new work must be set within certain time limits. The usual result is the establishment of rates before the methods have been standardized, operators have been trained to acceptable performance levels, and tooling has been satisfactorily developed. A brief study of the various improvement curves included in Chapter 3 will disclose the extreme hazards of such a practice and the costly effect of freezing many incentives at the low performance levels inherent in the beginning of a new product or production run. Unless there is unusually careful administration and auditing of rates, the standard times developed under initial conditions remain in effect long after significant improvements have been developed. The company's cost structure is then frozen at a high level, and another standard has been added to the list of loose and out of line rates.

In addition to the training allowances described in Chapter 3, a solution to this problem is the establishment of temporary rates. However, if the rates are not precanceled and clearly marked with the cancellation date, there is a very great tendency for them to become accepted as permanent rates and frozen into the cost structure.

Attempts to Restrict Rate Revisions

A long-standing union policy is that new methods are the only justification for rate changes. As a result, practically every union contract that contains a wage incentive section has a paragraph relating to the adjustment of rates due to methods changes. The following is typical of such paragraphs:

> If a change in design methods, equipment, tools, job duties or material makes an appreciable difference in the time required to perform the job, a revision may be made in the rate. If the change clearly affects definite elements in the existing job, only the elements affected will be changed. If a job has been so completely changed that a comparison between the old job and the new job is not reasonably possible, a restudy of the entire job may be made to establish the rate.

A similar paragraph in which the nature of the changes is more clearly defined is this one:

> Established standards and rates will remain in effect for the life of the contract unless there is a change in methods, procedures, feeds, speeds, dies, machines, jigs, fixtures, products, job conditions, or materials that tends to increase or decrease production. In these cases a restudy will be made and only the elements affected by the change will be adjusted.

There is no valid argument against the intent of these sample clauses or in the underlying philosophy. The difficulty lies in their administration:

1. The inherent thinking supporting such clauses is that each work element is a discrete, well-defined unit and changes affecting that element do not affect other elements. This view neglects the effect of overlapping elements or changes in work patterns resulting from elimination of or changes in an element.

2. The premise of the clauses is that such changes are specific and can be recognized prior to study. This view completely neglects the effect of minor creeping changes that are imperceptible in their effect except over fairly long periods of time.

3. The clauses require exact definition of each element not only in the new study but in the prior study. When old studies do not define elements completely, it is frequently difficult or impossible to prove a change.

EFFECT OF TIME LAPSE

Another administrative difficulty lies in the fact that specific changes are often unrecognized or unreported until long after they have occurred. The time lapse increases the difficulty of making the proper adjustment. The union may argue with some merit that, since the company did not adjust the rate at the time of the change, it abrogated or at least impaired its rights to make such an adjustment. (In this connection, John Waddleton, general counsel for Allis-Chalmers Manufacturing Company, puts some importance on "when" versus "where." In discussing the conditions under which rates may be changed as a result of changes in methods, he states that *when* implies an immediate change and that *where* is preferable because it does not connote immediacy.) A sample union clause that recognizes the effect of changes is furnished by Douglas Stern, chief industrial engineer of the Neenah Foundry Company:

When [where] a permanent incentive standard has been established on an operation, it shall not be changed because the employees through their individual skills and efforts develop incentive earnings in excess of the anticipated level, but shall only be changed for a clerical error or an error in computation. Any standard shall become inapplicable and subject to replacement or revision when [where] there has been a change in method including but not limited to: a change in crew size (in the case of the group incentive plan), motion pattern, materials, processes, layout, tools, jigs, or fixtures, or an accumulation of any changes which in total affects the time standard by 2 percent or more, provided that this percentage limitation shall not interfere with the sound use of standard data. It is recognized that some delay may occur between the time of occurrence of change of method and the establishment of revised standard. No such delay shall serve to limit or extinguish the company's right to establish a new standard. Employees are expected to meet acceptable quality standards and safety regulations, to take proper care of their equipment and to make proper utilization of materials.

This paragraph has several noteworthy features. It recognizes the use of standard data, the possibility of delays between the occurrence of a change and the establishment of the new standard, and also changes in quality standards as valid reasons for changing a standard.

Occasionally a union contract will contain a clause that has the effect of continuing an obsolete standard until a new standard is adopted. That can lead to serious trouble, particularly if there are delays in the adoption or acceptance of the revised standard. A clause covering the situation should read substantially as follows:

> If there is a change in method or conditions which changes the standard time by at least 5 percent, the existing standard will become inapplicable and a new standard will be established to replace it as soon as practical.

CREEPING CHANGES

All of the clauses reproduced here relate to specific, easily recognized changes. However, they do not adequately provide for the revisions in rates made necessary by creeping changes, of which the following are examples.

• A machine tool manufacturer carefully ground, filled in minor irregularities, sanded, and applied a coat of primer to incoming castings of major components. Over a number of years, improved quality control at the supplying foundry, as well as elimination of suppliers who had habitually supplied poor-quality castings, greatly changed the work requirement of preliminary treatment of castings. However, the nature of the work made it impossible to standardize all elements of the operation and, furthermore, there was still considerable variation in the quality of the castings between lots. Over a period of several years, the rates became hopelessly outdated.

• Over a period of time, improved quality control procedures resulted in fabricated parts coming to an assembly department with greatly reduced variations in tolerances. This in turn required much less shimming, or reduced the choice of shim sizes, and resulted in greatly reduced assembly times.

• Better alignment of parts due to improved fixturing or the use of new dies for fabricated steel parts greatly reduced filing and fitting times or time spent on alignment before fastening in final assembly.

• Obscure changes in grinding wheels very substantially improved performance in cleaning castings and also on precision grinding equipment.

• Improved tool life through such obscure changes such as improved coolants or metallurgical changes in the part meant that tools could be used for an entire day instead of having to be ground every hour.

• A time study man unwittingly allowed manual times for filing rough edges on parts being machined, but the operator subsequently performed the filing during the machine cycle. (This involves a nice technical point: Is it a change in method, an instance of operator ingenuity, or a time study man's error?)

• In the lathe department of a medium-sized plant, after receiving an assignment, the operator had to locate the particular skid containing the parts on which he was to work; that is, there was no specified area for incoming materials at the work center. Sometimes the skid of materials would be placed almost next to the operator's machine; at other times it was necessary for the operator to look in various areas before he located his skid. Frequently he had to move several skids in order to get his own skid from its location and to his machine. In that event, the time study man dutifully noted the time required to bring the material to the workplace and allocated that time as a noncyclic element and included it in the standard. On similar operations when no such time was required, none was allowed. Thus the allowances for material handling were extremely sporadic and depended entirely on conditions existing at the time of the particular study.

Sometime later the company instituted an improved production control system and as a result work in process was reduced materially. This in turn substantially reduced the physical amount of material waiting to be worked on in the department. Subsequently, definite spaces were allocated so that all incoming material was conveniently stored in a location central to the work center. But for the standards department to make the proper corrections among hundreds of sporadic and varying time allowances scattered over various time studies in the existing rate files was a practical impossibility.

These seven examples illustrate the extreme difficulty of properly maintaining a correct and equitable wage structure under the typical methods change clause in most union contracts. The only answer to the problem is the establishment of a thoroughly planned, frequent, and systematic audit of the entire incentive structure. Such a program will require major changes in the thinking of both top management and unions. That the program is being carried out in a small but increasing number of plants is a hopeful sign that, in the long run, industry will be able to control and modernize its wage incentive plans. Modifications of methods changes clauses should include the provision that such changes will be based on periodic audits. A sample clause might read as follows:

> Rates will be revised when the following are found to exist:
> Changes in method, tooling or fixtures, materials, processes, or
> job conditions or as a result of measurable changes in quality
> requirements or quality levels either of incoming parts or within
> the operation itself, or when there are measurable changes in
> such services as material handling, tool supplying, tool life, or
> similar service functions.
>
> Incentive rate changes as outlined above will be based on a specific
> audit procedure in which operations and standard data to be
> audited will be studied in exactly the same manner as when new
> rates are to be set. Audits will be made on a planned program
> based on the average total man-hours per year spent on the opera-
> tion, but in no case at intervals of longer than twelve months.
> Changes in incentives or on standard data made as a result of
> such audits are subject to the grievance procedures and all perti-
> nent data relating to such changes will be made available to the
> union representatives on request.

Such audit procedures are discussed in Chapter 13.

ADVANCE UNION APPROVAL OF STANDARDS

As noted previously, the development of a standard is a professional and technical function. Proper development of the standard
may frequently involve reference to similar operations, similar elements, and standard data to obtain the best consistency of a new
standard with existing standards for similar or comparable work. Approval of a standard by a union steward who is not conversant with
all of the techniques involved in its development becomes meaningless
and merely invites issues for further bargaining. Unsatisfactory earnings on a disputed rate are no measure of rate correctness. What
is most important is the consistency of the rate with proven rates
involving the same or comparable work content.

GRIEVANCE PROCEDURES

Many contracts are based on the use of union time study stewards.
Although that may be distasteful to many management-oriented people, it is usually quite reasonable in actual practice, particularly if
the union time study stewards are well trained in the company's

procedures in work measurement. If they are, a competent union man and an objective company man can usually work out satisfactory solutions to a grievance on a completely factual basis. In actual practice, most union time study stewards usually end up as time study engineers on the company payroll. They have the advantage of intimate knowledge of shop operations in addition to the technical training received by the company's industrial engineers. In most cases they are completely objective in their approach to work measurement.

Modification of Existing Contracts

Any discussion of restrictive clauses in most union contracts must ultimately lead to a discussion of how to eliminate or modify the clauses. Basically they can be eliminated only by following the procedures by which they were originally inserted into the contract, namely, collective bargaining. Any program directed toward the elimination of restrictive clauses must involve two phases. The first is the development of the proper top management policy toward the incentive function and the proper industrial engineering capability to administer wage incentives. The second is the development of a climate of mutual respect and confidence between the union and the company. Highly restrictive wage incentive clauses are generally an indication of serious malfunctioning of the wage incentive currently in existence, and they are frequently indicative of the union's attempt to protect itself from real or imagined abuses of the plan.

Management must somehow establish union confidence that the new plan will be sound, will be fairly administered, and will be kept up to date. Such a climate cannot be established by simple declarations of policy from top management; it must be reflected in day-to-day industrial engineering procedures, including prompt attention to and equitable adjustment of any existing incentive problems. That does not necessarily mean that concessions must be made to the union on each individual grievance or incentive problem. It does mean that prompt and careful attention will be given to the complaints concerning incentives that may be presented, that there will be a willingness to freely discuss all available data and other necessary information relating to rate problems, and that an attempt will be made to develop fair settlements consistent with sound industrial engineering policies. Until such a climate exists, there is no point in trying to remove objectionable incentive clauses at the bargaining table.

The bargaining process involves convincing the union that the proposed modifications of the incentive plan and broadening of the approach toward work measurement are in the best long-term interests of both the company and the union. It must be shown that these changes will improve the company's competitive position, which in the long run provides job security, and extend the incentive coverage in existence to a broader portion of the work force, both direct and indirect. That having been done, the actual bargaining process of eliminating the restrictive clauses becomes a matter of horse trading.

The horse-trading process may involve such things as a review of the job evaluation system so that the system will be compatible with proposed new levels of incentive gains. There is also the possibility of trading a general wage increase for improvements in the contract. Sometimes there is a possibility of a simple cash buy-out. The price may be high, but the alternative costs are usually still higher; they may not only limit productivity under the existing incentive plan but also prevent any extension of the plan to areas not presently covered. The increases in productivity through the application of proper incentives to previously unmeasured areas may represent savings to the company that will enhance its competitive situation and in some cases assure its survival in a highly competitive economy. In addition, employees presently on daywork may receive the advantages of incentive earnings, and that is often a strong selling point in dealing with the union.

It is beyond the scope of this book to do more than outline the general approach and broad strategy to be used in a bargaining situation. The best specific procedures to be followed will depend on many factors, including the general climate of relationships between the company and the union, the severity of existing incentive problems and the specific needs for correction, the labor content in the firm's cost structure, and the firm's competitive position. All these considerations will necessarily dictate the tactics to be used in attempting to improve a union contract.

The complex nature of wage incentive clauses and the effect of the clauses not only on the proper functioning of the wage incentive plan but also on the company's entire labor cost structure make this area of negotiation much too important to be delegated to persons not completely knowledgeable in the field. The details of wage incentive clauses should not be handled by the industrial relations staff or company attorneys without the advice and counsel of the chief industrial engineer or his equivalent. He is the one who is acquainted with all of the incentive problems in the plant and is aware of the lasting harm done by many seemingly innocuous wage incentive clauses.

There is a regrettable tendency for management people on the bargaining committee to accept clauses proposed by the union if they appear to be part of a local pattern. That is a dangerous approach. The applicability of specific contract clauses should be judged by the suitability of the clauses to the individual company situation and its problems, and not on their acceptance by other industries whose conditions may be entirely different.

If the standards department is sizable enough to have a chief industrial engineer, he should be a permanent member of the management bargaining team. He has the responsibility for directing much of the money spent on labor and is in a position to point out the dangers of seemingly harmless clauses. If he is to direct the wage incentive function, he should have the background of the entire bargaining relationship between the company and the union. In addition, his presence at the bargaining table emphasizes his status in the company and helps create respect for the proper conduct of the wage incentive function.

UNION-MANAGEMENT RELATIONS

There is a direct relation between good management and good union relations; at least there is in the small and medium-sized plants, in which there are more direct communications between top management and employees. On the other hand, in most small and medium-sized plants in which there are poor union relations, there is usually much evidence of intransigent and inept management. The industrial climate is then characterized by a complete lack of respect or confidence between the parties, attempts to hedge the union contract with innumerable protective clauses, and an accumulation of unresolved grievances unhappily awaiting a legalistic approach to their resolution.

Such situations are never resolved by the publication of pious industrial relations statements by top management. The climate can be changed only by sound improvement in working relations based on reasonable, prompt, and correct decisions by the line supervisors and by the recognition that, in many situations, both sides of the bargaining table have some merit to their arguments. When management, from top level down to the foreman on the floor, has been able to maintain and develop not only good manufacturing policies but good personal relationships with employees, stewards, and union officers—and has been able to create a climate of mutual respect and confidence—union leadership is usually responsible and intelligent and union-management relations are basically sound.

In the long run, good management heightens the appeal of the union politician who is intent on battling management for maximum gains to his constituents. Good management does not mean giving in to the union on all points and granting all its requests. Rather, it means a coordinated agreement on sound basic principles, from top management to foreman level, coupled with the recognition that the other side occasionally has some good ideas. Good common sense applied to contract interpretations is preferable to a narrow legalistic interpretation of the meanings of the various paragraphs.

11

Modernizing the Plan

THE INFORMATION OBTAINED from evaluations and audits of a wage incentive plan and its administration forms a sound basis for modernizing the plan. However, a modernization program cannot be formulated and carried out at the standards level alone.

Role of Top Management

First of all, top management must develop its own policies and its own objectives in the area of wage incentive administration. It must agree wholeheartedly with and be willing to support the basic concept of incentives. It must accept the idea that more pay can result only from more work, more effort, or more skill and that the person who does not have more skill or who does not want to put forth the extra effort is not entitled to additional pay above the base wage.

Furthermore, management must have the confidence that the industrial engineering techniques that it employs are sound and correctly administered, and it must be willing to audit the program frequently enough to support that confidence. Management must then have the courage to back up its standards department and use the data that the department develops.

Top management in a concern that is having difficulties with wage incentives frequently concludes that it can solve its problems by going to measured daywork. The conclusion is naive; switching incentive plans does not correct basic administrative deficiencies. If the shop administration cannot make a wage incentive plan work satisfactorily, it is no better qualified to operate the shop effectively under measured daywork.

The usual result of changing from incentives to measured daywork is to pay the equivalent of incentive wages for daywork performance or less and to have a substantial increase in direct labor costs and often seriously reduced levels of output as well. In this connection, Harvey J. Tadewald, Manager of Industrial Engineering at John Deere and Company, Moline, Illinois, stated in a lecture that if his company were to abandon its existing incentive plans, it would, in his opinion, need a substantial amount of additional facilities, equipment, and employees to maintain the same level of production.

Therefore, the first step in modernizing a wage incentive plan is to establish basic principles and objectives and put them in writing: the philosophy of the plan or plans and the general conditions under which standards will be developed, the procedures by which they will be audited, and the conditions under which they will be revised. The statement should also outline the policy relating to the use of either individual or group incentives, the method of computing earnings (daily, weekly, or by the job), and, in particular, how lost time is to be handled. Appendix A is an example of this type of general statement.

Development of a Program

The next step involves the development of a program for corrective action. It should be based on the findings of audits and samplings as outlined in preceding chapters. The program should outline proper corrective action required to:

1. Bring existing standards into line as needed.
2. Whenever possible, extend incentives to areas not presently covered.
3. Correct shop recording and timekeeping deficiencies if indicated.
4. Bring about proper incentive administration at foreman level if it is needed.
5. Establish definite time limits and assignment of responsibilities for the program.

When the program is completed, it is vitally important that good communications be observed and that the entire program be thoroughly discussed at all management levels as well as with proper union officials. Techniques for dealing with the union are discussed later in this chapter.

General Earnings Objectives

One of the most common symptoms of an outmoded plan is unusually high incentive earnings. Under such circumstances the tendency of management is to resist any upward pressure on the base wage structure, and so a discussion of the proper relationship between the base wages and incentive earnings is important. In many situations with runaway incentive plans, there is a tendency on the part of the company to hold down the hourly wage structure on the theory that unusually high incentive earnings will make up for low base wages. However, the byproducts of such a policy are these:

• The difficulty of recruiting qualified employees to begin work with the company. Most new employees are characteristically more interested in the starting wage than they are in the prospects of high incentive earnings at some future date.

• The extreme difficulty of holding and attracting employees in the higher skills such as maintenance and toolmaking, for whom there may be no incentive opportunity.

• An unusually great pressure on the company, because of the disparity between incentive earnings and daywork, to institute some type of guaranteed earnings policy for employees who may be transferred from incentive work to non-incentive work. Yet to do so would be to further weaken the entire incentive plan.

THE IDEAL WAGE STRUCTURE

The ideal wage structure for a company should be based on careful job descriptions and job evaluation so as to maintain the proper relationship between various occupational groups. The basic wage pattern developed from the job evaluations should have the following characteristics:

• It should compare favorably with area (or in the case of large corporations, national) wages paid for the same or similar occupations on a non-incentive basis.

• The ideal range between minimum wages for the lowest-skilled occupations and the wages for top-skilled occupations should be at least in the ratio of 1:1.5 and preferably 1:2. For example, if a sweeper is paid $2 per hour, the wages of a skilled toolmaker should approach $4 per hour as a minimum.

Most area surveys indicate an approximate straight-line relationship between job evaluation points and base wages up to or slightly beyond the midpoint of the entire range. From there on, in most cases, the base wages seem to increase at a somewhat greater rate. That is probably because labor in the higher-skilled occupational categories is relatively scarce and therefore has a somewhat higher dollar value per point of job evaluation. It can also be construed that part of the increase is due to the upward pressure on earnings because the higher-skilled occupations are generally non-incentive. The curves of Figures 20 and 21 summarize typical area wage surveys for non-incentive workers in Wisconsin and Connecticut. Both curves have

Figure 20. Typical daywork wages in Wisconsin.

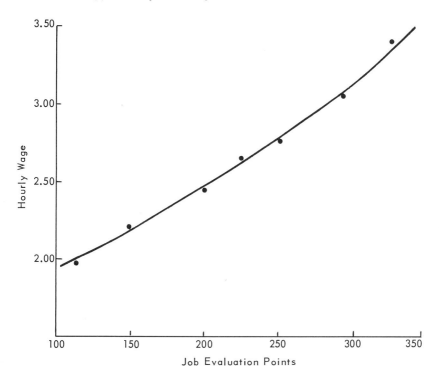

Figure 21. Typical daywork wages in Connecticut.

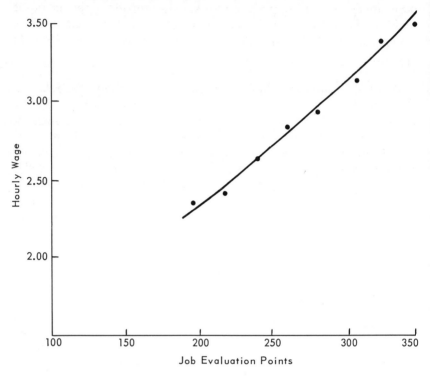

an increase in slope—that is, an increase in values—at the upper ends of the scale as discussed here.

In summary, the base wage structure should be consistent with area wages for similar occupations. Base wages must also be competitive within the industry, and with the national ranges in skilled classifications such as toolmakers. Furthermore, it should compensate for normal levels of activity. Pay for performance above that considered as normal is a function of the incentive plan.

ELIMINATION OF INEQUITIES

A characteristic symptom of an incentive plan in difficulty is inequities between earnings in various work centers or occupational groups. Frequently, by reason of loose incentives, unskilled workers may be earning more than those in the higher-skilled occupations. Correction of this difficulty will frequently involve serious adjustments to individual earnings. Such changes can no longer be made unilaterally; they are bargainable items, and union involvement becomes necessary. Union participation in incentive modifications may be distasteful to many management people, but it is frequently an asset because union representatives often have an extremely detailed knowledge of the shortcomings of existing systems. Union participation in modifications of an existing system has several other advantages, particularly if it can be developed in an atmosphere of genuine effort to solve a mutual problem.

Union representatives frequently are in a position to make practical suggestions. In addition, their participation in the development of new plans can only improve the possibility of plan acceptance by employees. The secret of success in this type of venture is to separate union participation in incentive modification from the grievance and bargaining procedures. If possible, union representation should include individuals who are not involved in handling grievances or in collective bargaining. These joint committees can have quite rewarding and profitable results, but the atmosphere must be one of mutual respect and willingness to listen to opinions of other people.

In non-union plants, it is frequently possible to arrange for employee representation by selection of certain key employees who have demonstrated natural leadership in their groups and who can be depended upon to help communicate management thinking to the rank-and-file employees. Assuming that the existing plan has so deteriorated that it must be completely revamped, there are several approaches.

If the base wage structure is low and the ratio of incentive gains is too high, a very common procedure is to combine incentive revisions with a new job evaluation program that will realistically set base wages at area levels and simultaneously introduce new incentives that will develop more realistic incentive gains. Such a plan can be so calculated as to protect the take-home pay of the employees, that is, the higher base wage coupled with the lower incentive gains produces the same hourly earnings.

EXAMPLE OF THOROUGHGOING REVIEW

In an instance of unusually distorted incentive gains coupled with low and inconsistent base wages, recognition of the situation by both company and union produced the following paragraph in a contract renegotiation.

Article 25   Earnability Study

The Union and Management jointly recognize the need for review of job base rates and production time standards to produce a better relationship of earnings with regard to skill, effort and work measurements.

The parties therefore agree that such review will be undertaken in the early stages of the life of this Agreement in order that early implementation of a mutually acceptable plan may be accomplished.

In keeping with the intent of this clause, the company engaged the services of management consultants in the area of work measurement and wage incentives, who subsequently offered a program in which the union agreed to participate:

1. The establishment and training of a group of standards engineers in modern methods of work measurement by the consultants.
2. A complete restudy by the engineers and consultants of all incentive rates in the plant based on median expected earning attainments of 30 percent.
3. A complete restudy and job evaluation effort to be conducted by a committee consisting of four members from the union representing each of the two plants in the city, three members of management, and the consultant acting as chairman. A secretary, selected by the committee, was to be responsible for taking minutes and distributing copies to both union and management.

The basic level of take-home wages had been arrived at in the existing contract. Prior agreement on the complete program delegated the following responsibilities to the committee:

General Wage Levels. Any plans for a new wage structure and incentive plan are to recognize existing labor costs; in other words, the committee is not negotiating a wage increase or a wage decrease. The committee is to follow a formula based on a given number of employees of given skills accepted as a model for the plants, and for a normal product mix; the total labor value is to be virtually the same with the new system as it would be with the present system.

Procedures. The general procedure to be followed by the committee is as follows:

1. Decide on factors to be used in the evaluation procedure.
2. Agree on descriptions for each factor.
3. Assign point values for each factor.
4. Have the consultant work with the foremen involved to develop a master list of all job classifications for review by the committee.
5. Job evaluation.
    a. Decide on sequence of work centers to cover.
    b. Schedule meetings with foremen, steward, employees involved, and consultant.
    c. In cooperation with parties named in (b), write rough job descriptions.
6. Review job descriptions with committee.
7. Assign point values for each factor.
8. After approving them, have job descriptions and point evaluations reviewed by the appropriate shop stewards.
9. Develop a spread sheet for consistency.
10. Have the consultant then: (a) Determine a typical mix of jobs (occupations) at the company. (b) Determine the present cost for this mix of jobs including current labor rates, current average incentive gains, and current coverage. (c) By using the data of (b), develop a point wage curve to provide a specific base wage for each occupation and to reflect the current cost of labor, fit properly to the restraints of contract minimum wages, area wage structures, and current peg points, and also to reflect median expected incentive gains to be developed through the new wage incentives being studied.
11. The mathematical analysis of (10) is then to be reviewed and approved by the committee. Upon completion of this portion of the assignment, the consultant will develop complete job evaluation manuals for use both by the union and the company and arrange for indoctrinating sessions to be carried on with the various foremen and shop stewards.

While the new job evaluation structure was being developed, the consultant's staff was actively studying all incentive rates, assisting in selecting and training standards department personnel in proper work measurement procedures, and establishing an up-to-date file of standards for all direct operations. On completion of the new base wage structure and its ratification by the union, both the new incentives and the new base wages were installed simultaneously. The old system was discontinued.

Union Involvement. Usually in the operation of such a program several meetings are needed to establish an objective relationship between the various union and management members. Objectivity is gained as the various individuals learn to work together to solve common problems. Since neither of the parties is discussing specific grievances or contract clauses, the conversation soon tends to become more relaxed and informal and constructive suggestions come from both sides. The degree of union involvement in the program cited was relatively great because of the somewhat unusual circumstances:

1. There was no rational pattern to the earnings profiles for various occupations. Both the base wage structure and the incentive structure were so distorted and inconsistent that it was found to be impossible to correct either one without making compatible modifications in the other.

2. An earlier attempt to install job evaluation had failed because of rejection of the plan by the union. The rejection pointed out two very important facts: (a) The negative union attitude toward a job evaluation could be resolved only by increasing union participation in the job evaluation effort. (b) Modifications of the base wage structure would have to be made simultaneously with compatible modifications in the incentive plan.

3. Because of the intermixing of improper wages and improper incentive rates and the relatively low rate of obsolescence of manufacturing operations, it would have been impractical to protect present levels of earnings to certain individuals by red circling either rates or wages. Because a system of job bidding by seniority was in effect, skilled operators would often bid for relatively unskilled jobs in specific situations that involved unusually lucrative incentive earnings.

4. Because of all of these factors, it was impossible to make any statements to the union agreeing to protect present earnings to individuals and it was impossible for the company to guarantee that "nobody would get hurt." The only guarantee that the company could conscientiously make was that, for a given mix of work and for a given mix of occupational groups, total labor costs under the proposed method would be identical with those under the existing method. Considerable time, patience, and numerous meetings were needed to sell the idea to the union. It was necessary to emphasize that to continue the original procedures would be to perpetuate the chaotic earnings structure and that that would be a definite competitive handicap to the company.

The situation described here, an extreme one, was presented in some detail to indicate the very complex situations involved in overhauling and modernizing a wage incentive plan.

HORSE TRADING TO RESOLVE INEQUITIES

Fortunately, most situations are considerably simpler than the one described. Sometimes the horse-trading approach may solve some of the more simple incentive distortions. A case in point is a non-union cosmetics plant. Various employee groups had expressed dissatisfaction with individual incentive rates. A thorough study of an agreed-upon group of operations indicated that there were inequities. Both loose rates and tight rates were found.

The rates were adjusted to develop a satisfactory level of median incentive earnings. Results of the time studies and all details were thoroughly discussed with the employees and their foreman. The modified rates were then adopted. Fortunately, in this particular situation, good top management and good shop supervision were present. The net result was a successful adjustment, as evidenced by the results of an NLRB-supervised representation election that had been requested by a union. The election was held several months after the rates were modified, and the union was rejected by a substantial majority of the employees.

The approach to the cosmetics plant problem was suitable because of low process obsolescence. An approach to review and modernization of existing rates in a non-union medium-sized electronic components plant is the systematic selection of work centers to be thoroughly audited and the updating of all rates as part of a long-range program. The changes resulting from the audits might be either increases or decreases in the standards. The proposed changes are carefully discussed with the employees affected, and the results of the time study and all pertinent data are reviewed in detail.

Once a given work center is audited, the audit procedure is moved to another work center in accordance with the schedule. The planned program has resulted in a uniform and consistent wage incentive structure based on qualified plant industrial engineering assistance. It has brought to light serious weaknesses in past procedures. Existing files of time studies were inadequate and poorly documented. They had been made by various individuals prior to the development of a definite wage incentive policy and procedure.

The overall results of the program have been quite satisfactory. Many inequities have been eliminated from the incentive structure. The climate now is one of excellent employee relations furthered by highly capable top management.

When a wage plan has so deteriorated that a complete new plan must be substituted, the acceptance of a new plan may require skillful bargaining. The horse-trading function may involve an overall wage increase as a trade-off for agreement on a major incentive revision. Sometimes a flat cash payment to the affected employees may be required to make the revision palatable.

Union-Management Committees

The operation of union-management committees merits some discussion. First, the details of the base wage structure and the incentive system are now universally recognized as negotiable items and cannot be kept out of the bargaining area. However, the operation of a job evaluation system or of a wage incentive plan within basic and agreed-on policies is definitely a function of management. Determinations relating to specific cases cannot be left to mutual agreement. Problems relating to the day-to-day issuance of incentive rates or specific wage decisions are a part of the grievance procedure and should remain there. The value of a joint committee lies in:

- Making available detailed knowledge of the working of incentives at the shop level.
- Contributing to the planning of major revisions to incentives.
- Planning for an extension of an existing plan into new areas.
- Generally reviewing performance under the plan.
- Exchanging useful information and policies.
- Discussing overall problems without the stress of the grievance committee or the heat of the bargaining table.

Effect of Committee on Rank and File

Another important value of such a committee is that any decisions, policies, or procedures arrived at by it will have a much greater degree of acceptance by the rank and file of employees than if those same actions were arrived at unilaterally. Thus, the committee performs a valuable function as a communication medium in the selling of new plans and proposals to the employee body. The committee thus becomes an informal medium for discussion of proposed changes and modifications in wage and incentive plans and can often be used to test or discuss proposed developments before any commitments are made.

The same means are available for discussion with employee groups in non-union plants. Unfortunately, the channels of communication to the people affected are not as well defined. With the lack of formal communication, there is much greater possibility of misinterpretation and failure to notify all people involved. Informal shop committees composed of representative employees who have shown leadership ability and who are recognized by the other employees may be very helpful.

Although such committees can make valuable contributions in the area of good union relations, they do require a climate of mutual confidence and respect. When such a climate exists, it can be improved through work with a joint committee. If it does not exist, no number of meetings or revisions of procedures or systems will supply the confidence and mutual respect that must underlie any attempt at union-management cooperation.

USE OF CONSULTANT

In any situation involving the broad-scale revision of both base wages and incentives, the use of a qualified outside consultant has numerous advantages. Management receives the advice and counsel of a professional who has gained experience in the same areas from earlier assignments. An objective approach by a qualified third party will often reveal underlying problems affecting the interplay of incentives and wages that will not be apparent to the local operating staff. A consultant can make a sound evaluation not only of the shortcomings of a specific situation but also of the capacity of both the technical staff and the shop management to administer any new system that might be developed.

From the standpoint of the union, the presence of an experienced professional is an advantage in that it subjects any new plans to an impartial review that will consider the long-range interests of both the company and the union. A consultant who is skilled in communications has much to gain from his work with union officers in discovering not only the more apparent defects of the incentive plan but also the defects that are not as easily recognized. The fact that a new plan has been developed and reviewed with a third party helps union officers sell the merits of the plan to their people. Also, from his previous experience, the consultant has frequently built a reputation of credibility in union circles.

Another advantage in using outside professional help is that a management that has been unable to develop, properly administer, or control and maintain its wage incentive plan can scarcely be expected to develop the resources to perform a complete overhaul of the plan without some outside guidance. Top management may frequently require firm and objective counsel in the development of its policies and administrative procedures. Such counsel is difficult for the local standards staff to provide.

It is possible that a new plan may require a much higher level of skill in the industrial engineering effort than is locally available. It may require the upgrading, training, or employing of new industrial engineering talent that can be effectively accomplished with the assistance of outsiders. Not only can the consultant assist in the selection and training of personnel, but arrangements can usually be made for him to periodically review progress and attainments under the new plan.

12

A Modernization Program

In any program involving the modernization of a wage incentive plan, the establishment of the right to audit and to use proper auditing procedures is a major consideration. Management has the inherent right to audit of all its operating procedures, and the wage incentive function should be no exception. We have noted previously that union contracts tend to increase the rigidity of the wage incentive structure even though manufacturing processes are in a continual state of change, usually one of improvement.

The benefits of increased productivity should ideally be made available not only to labor but also to the customer and to the owners. To permit benefits to accrue to labor alone would be unjust to both the customer and the owners and, in the long run, detrimental to labor itself. Most of the changes that result in increased productivity are management-instituted—the result of improved equipment, better tooling, improved quality control of incoming parts, methods engineering, and better material handling.

Establishing the Right to Audit

In Chapter 10 it was pointed out that practically all union contracts recognize methods changes as variously defined as the sole legitimate reason for revising an incentive rate. It was also pointed out that although that approach is adequate to adjust for major substantive changes, it is completely inadequate to adjust for minor improvements or for improvements that are not measurable except over a fairly long period of time. Furthermore, procedures for reporting methods changes are generally unorganized and inadequate in most concerns. Therefore, the periodic audit is about the only practical way to maintain wage incentives and minimize the problems outlined in Chapter 11. That fact is recognized by many progressive organizations, with the result that the auditing function is becoming increasingly important in the well-organized standards department. However, union recognition of the right to audit is lacking in practically all union contracts in existence today.

The challenge to management, therefore, is to establish the right to audit within existing union contracts at the earliest possible opportunity. That may be difficult, but it should seldom be impossible. The best approach is through the amplification of the change-in-method section of the wage incentive clauses. An important step in the initiation of the auditing procedure is to establish the right to audit as a means of discovering and evaluating methods changes on a systematic basis. Practically all union officials will agree that it is highly desirable to maintain consistency in the rate structure and eliminate inequities, so that approach to the audit function is the logical one. The stipulation that rates will go up or down as indicated by the audit should help to sell most union officials on the principle of auditing. Most union officials are inclined to accept a program that will insure that the occasional tight rate will be loosened. A clause that recognizes methods changes and the right to audit is given in Chapter 10.

Organizing the Audit Activity

The right to audit having been established, the next step is the proper organization of the activity within the standards department. Auditing must be recognized by both the standards staff and top management as an important and continuing function. It should not be relegated to a group of staff members as something to be done when there is time available. As a continuing function, it must be supported by proper allocation of staff manpower.

Ideally, assignments to the audit function should be limited to the most experienced members of the standards staff. The challenge to the auditor is much greater than the challenge to the engineer who is developing new standards or standard data. Successful auditing requires a broad background in work measurement, a thorough grounding in shop practices, a complete knowledge of the rate structure within the organization, and good personal acceptance on the shop floor. Another requirement is tact and good judgment when dealing with factors that may include intangibles. Those are the minimum requirements for staff members assigned to auditing. Staff members who have achieved recognition for fairness and credibility in their dealings with shop personnel are at a considerable advantage.

Obviously, it is only the larger standards departments that will have enough manpower to permit full-time assignments to the audit function. A smaller department will have to allocate its man-hours to auditing as best it can but on the principle that auditing is as important as setting new standards. In the case of the small department, a certain number of audits should be planned every week and on completion should be reported to top management for review. Neither pressure from the shop to secure maximum coverage nor special assignments to the standards group should be permitted to reduce the time allocated to auditing. It is in this area that the industrial engineer or his counterpart is dependent on top management for adequate support of the auditing function.

Auditing Procedures

Standards to be audited can be scheduled in a number of ways; the best method will depend to some extent on the manner in which work is scheduled in the shop. Several ways are outlined in Chapter 9. In most cases after the operation or operations to be audited are selected, the procedures will follow closely those used in establishing new standards. The auditor should use shop courtesy in making his presence and purpose known to foreman, operator, and also the union steward if one is involved. The normal pattern of time study procedures in use in the shop should be followed.

When he has completed the study and has obtained all the necessary data relating to the operation, the auditor should remove the old time studies and standards from the files for a review and comparison. If there is no significant difference between the standard in effect and the one indicated by the audit, the audit studies, properly dated, can be filed with the old studies. If there are card files for use in recording audit information, the cards can be marked when the audit is completed and refiled under the next date for audit.

If significant differences have been discovered in the audit, procedures should be the same as those followed when new standards are issued, except that the revised standards should not be issued to the shop before a complete review with the foreman and employees affected has been made. For that review all the information concerning the necessity for change must be made available. Communication with those affected is important in maintaining the credibility of the audit function. Each significant change between the old standard and the audit standard requires careful explanation and factual information about the nature of any changes that have occurred. If the information is not made available carefully, tactfully, and with sound judgment, the entire auditing program is endangered. It is very easy to create hostility by proposing changes that appear to be capricious and unsupported.

Auditing Standard Data. The regular auditing and maintenance of standard data has an even greater significance than the auditing of individual standards. Standard data are subject to the same factors of obsolescence and production improvements as individual rates are, but the significance of their obsolescence is even greater because hundreds and even thousands of rates may be derived from a single set of standard data. Therefore, it is important that the audit of any standard data in use be scheduled at more frequent intervals than the audit of individual rates.

The pattern for the review of standard data will vary considerably with the manner in which the standard data are used in the shop as well as with the frequency and extent of their use. The auditing procedure should be about the same as that for individual rates: The auditor should make a complete time study and gather all data pertinent to the particular operation being performed with rates set from standard data. The audit studies should then be referred to the original data or spread sheets used in developing the current standard data.

If no significant deviations are observed, the audit studies can then be filed with the basic data used in developing the standard data sheets. If there are variations, a thorough study of their range and extent is indicated. Here the suspicion is that the complete formulation may require updating. Any revisions must be reviewed by shop personnel in the same thorough manner as revisions in individual standards.

Role of the Foreman in Auditing. The foreman's role in supporting the audit function is as important as his part in administering wage incentives. He must be convinced by top management that his support of the wage incentive administration and its periodic auditing is of vital importance in keeping the system healthy. As noted earlier, in most shop organizations the foreman has the primary responsibility to report methods changes to the standards department. The audit does not relieve him of that responsibility; it may even point out his shortcomings in not reporting changes.

Effecting the Adjustments. When definite, clear-cut, and measurable methods changes occur, rates should be adjusted as quickly as possible. Every delay in adjustment increases the difficulty of the company in making the necessary revision. If several months go by with no revision to standards as a result of significant methods or tooling changes, the difficulty of rate revision is compounded. The delay infers that the company has acquiesced in the change without making the necessary rate revision.

Importance of Continuing Audits

The reader will note a great similarity in the audit procedures described here and those described in Chapters 7 and 8. The latter are designed largely to evaluate existing levels of performance of the standards department, the wage incentive administration in general, and the shop administration in particular. Audits of that type are usually best performed by someone not directly related to the standards or shop activities. They are designed primarily to evaluate performance of the standards department and the shop administration to determine whether corrective measures are necessary in either organization or to assist in determining basic incentive policies and improving procedures. That is the type of audit that might be expected to be made by a corporate industrial engineer visiting a branch plant or by a consultant retained to evaluate the various functions.

What concerns us here is a continuing type of audit that is designed to assure the maintenance of existing standards and their prompt adjustment to changes in the shop. The continuing audit is best performed by the standards department as a part of its incentive maintenance activity. The function thus becomes completely analogous to that of preventive maintenance of manufacturing equipment.

The continuing incentive audits are incomplete without a parallel continuing audit of the timekeeping and reporting system. In preceding chapters the importance of proper recording and reporting procedures and their close relationship with the health of the incentive system has been discussed. All of the good work of maintaining the system properly can be nullified if the reporting and recording system

Figure 22. Form for factory timekeeping audit.

Date _____
Dept. _____
Foreman _____
Audit by _____

Line No.	Operation Clock No.	Part No.	Operation No. Conformance	Specification Conformance	Rate Being Used	Rate in File	Method Conformance	Time Study Method Description	Recorded Count	Verified Count	Discrepancies	Remarks	Discussed with	Payroll Verification
1.														
2.														
3.														
4.														
5.														
6.														
7.														
8.														
9.														
10.														

General Comments
_____
_____
_____

Explanation of Timekeeping Audit

Operation clock number	Note clock number at time of observation.
Part number	Note from actual material in use.
Operation number	Note conformance of operation number with rate summary. Is unauthorized downtime being claimed?
Specification conformance	Do specification and actual work being done agree?
Rate being used	Note rate on operator's time slip.
Rate in file	Check file for conformance with rate being used.
Method conformance	Note method used by operators.
Time study method description	Is time study method description full and complete and does it conform with method used by operators?
Recorded count	Note count on operator's time slip.
Verified count	Verify actual count with operator's recorded count.
Discrepancies	Note and describe observed discrepancies.
Remarks	Note any unusual or unverified situations.
Discussed with	Discuss any discrepancies with foreman and note his initials.
Payroll verification	Verify all times, counts, and computations on operator's time slip with observations made; also with payroll entries.

is not closely controlled. Therefore, regular audits of that function are as important as audits of the incentive structure.

DESIRABLE AUDIT CHARACTERISTICS

Since in most plants the timekeeping department is an extension of the accounting department, it is preferable that it be audited by someone connected with the accounting function. That is particularly true because the accounting department is generally more familiar with the audit procedures required. These audits also should be performed as a continuing program. They should be developed on a random sampling basis to secure proper statistical validity. Audit points should include:

- Verification of counts.
- Verification of proper operation numbers and rate applications.
- Verification of proper starting and stopping times for the work being done.
- Complete spot checks to make sure that the operator is actually working on a specific operation covered by the account number that is indicated on his time ticket.
- Verification of proper controls for allowances such as lost time and waiting for material.

The audits should be performed on a completely random sampling basis so that there is no pattern of locations or departments. As in the incentive audit, the results of the audit—particularly any discrepancies found—must be thoroughly discussed with the foreman and the persons responsible for the timekeeping procedure. A type of audit sheet developed for the purpose, together with explanatory instructions, is shown in Figure 22.

In conclusion, it should be pointed out again that the two audits described in this chapter are completely analogous to accepted procedures used not only in preventive maintenance of mechanical equipment but also in the statistical control of product quality. Considering the effect of such controls on product cost, the incentive audit and timekeeping audit are equally important to basic cost control.

13

Upgrading the Standards Department

DURING THE LATE 1920s and the 1930s, the functions of time study and standards application were normally carried out by a rate setter. Traditionally, that individual had a desk in some corner of a shop office. His equipment consisted largely of a stopwatch, a time study board, a slide rule, a filing cabinet for his time studies, and a card file of hand-written rate cards covering work done in the area. His supervision and training were elementary. Probably in most cases his greatest asset was familiarity with the type of work being done in his area. Standard data were either lacking or rudimentary. If there were any at all, they were probably in the form of personal notebook entries of standard time for elements of operations common to the work being done in the area.

From that largely self-taught background very little could be expected in the way of innovation or new techniques. Extreme reliance on experience gained within the organization did little to encourage improvements or advancements beyond past practice. Also, at that time our educational institutions had practically nothing to offer students with an interest in time and motion study. Most of the textbooks on the subject were yet to be written.

Progress in
Industrial Engineering

Some progress was made in the 1930s, but there were few major changes in industrial engineering techniques prior to the sweep of unionization that occurred during the late 1930s and the 1940s. Most of the union contract clauses entered into at that time reflected the prevailing time study practices. With the unions strongly opposed to any liberalization of contract clauses, it is not surprising that many of those restrictive clauses are in today's contracts.

More recent years have seen tremendous improvement in the number and quality of industrial engineering curriculums. As a result, well-trained industrial engineers are now available to industry. Still more recent developments in computer aids and the newer statistical aids such as linear programming, operations research, and the use of multivariable and linear regression techniques have given the industrial engineer many new tools for use in his activities.

The young graduating industrial engineer is expected to be familiar with many of the newer developments, but he is frequently lacking in practical shop experience. For that reason, as noted in Chapter 7, the ideal standards department in a manufacturing institution of any magnitude should have a mixture of practical shop-trained technicians and industrial engineering graduates. Each has much to offer to the other if the environment is congenial to a recognition of the potential contributions of each individual.

Standards Department Size

Much discussion has been generated by the question of proper size of a standards department. From time to time, surveys have been conducted in an attempt to develop averages of the number of standards employees in relation to the number of hourly employees. Broad averages are of doubtful value. They do not take into consideration the nature of the work being done, the obsolescence of product or process, the amount of standard data in use, or the extent of incentive coverage achieved or desired. We have emphasized that there are four main functions of standards personnel in wage incentive administration: methods improvement, development of new standards, development of standard data, and maintenance of the rate structure. These four functions must be related to the overall long-range goals of the standards department. The questions that arise about those goals are the following:

- What are the long-range goals in developing standard data, increasing incentive coverage to new areas such as indirect labor, overhauling the wage incentive structure in outmoded areas, and developing and maintaining proper auditing procedures?
- What manpower is needed to attain the goals within the desired scheduled times?
- How effectively is the standards department meeting its objectives?

The manpower requirements of the standards department will depend largely on the answers to those questions. The same evaluation and analysis will be useful in the establishing of the proper mix of shop-trained and graduate standards personnel.

The Work Measurement Function

Traditionally, work measurement has been concerned largely with inputs: the elements of time required by various motion patterns, machining times, or carefully defined process times. The traditional concept is that all inputs are fixed elements to be standardized, controlled, and, ideally, prevented from varying beyond minimal ranges. The calculation of process variables, including machine times, has normally been limited to the use of simple algebraic formulas. Among the new approaches that have been made available to the work measurement function are:

1. Work sampling, whereby statistically determined patterns of random sampling can predict overall performance within demonstrable limits of accuracy. It is particularly useful in determining delay allowances.

2. Linear programming, which permits the optimum selections of work distributions for multiple activities.

3. Progress curves (also known as learning curves or improvement curves), which enable relatively close predictions of improvements in performance over extended periods of production.

4. Critical path method, which is a way to determine optimum program planning of related activities that require varying inputs of time and costs.

5. Multiple regression analysis (also called multivariant analysis), which permits the development of mathematical formulas for accurate evaluation of outputs controlled by multiple variables whose combined effect may obscure the individual relationship and may not be made apparent by application of conventional techniques.

6. Simulation, a technique of analysis whereby the effects of various changes in job conditions or characteristics can be rapidly simulated on the computer to aid in the selection of the optimum combinations of factors.

7. Analysis of variance, a tool that can be used to determine whether nonquantitative factors such as sex, department, and labor grade are significant in explaining differences in operator times, output, and quality.

8. Distribution analysis, a study of the frequency distribution of performance figures of different groups to analyze curve characteristics such as skewness due to incentive motivation and truncation due to coworker pressures.

The mathematical concepts that underlie these techniques were formerly understood only by the trained statistician, but they are now a part of practically all acceptable engineering courses. In addition, they are available in refresher courses or specialized seminars for the older practicing industrial engineers. The newer techniques represent a complete new array of measurement procedures that enable the industrial engineer to apply his skills to many areas formerly considered unmeasurable and thereby broaden the application of wage incentives.

COMPUTER APPLICATIONS

The advent of the computer has also expanded industrial engineering activities. Many of the newer statistical procedures, particularly multiple regression analysis, require extensive computations. The computer reduces the computational work and so makes available mathematical procedures that would otherwise be impractical.

There have been numerous attempts to develop computerized work measurement techniques, usually systems in which voluminous existing data are stored. Thus, they have largely been automations of existing clerical systems. The approach had two undesirable characteristics: It requires lengthy clerical description of method and selection of formulas that are to be applied by the computer, and the applications are of such nature that they require extensive computer stored data capacity. To overcome those disadvantages and to really

utilize the speed and efficiency of the modern computer in the genera-
tion of time standards, it has been necessary to develop new concepts
of the reasons for expenditure of time in industrial operations.

Two systems based on newer concepts have been developed by
Management Science, Inc., of Appleton, Wisconsin. The systems,
called UnivEl and UniForm, have been introduced into a wide variety
of industries with uniformly successful results.[1]

UnivEl. UnivEl is a method of work measurement based on a
biomechanical formula; normal standard times for operations are generated by means of a mathematical model stored in the computer.
Data are introduced to the computer by use of a simple numerical
code that is easy to learn and simple to apply. The computer translates
the simple coding plus descriptive names or phrases into a detailed
method instruction sheet and calculates the elemental and total times
including the pieces per hour that are expected. Its savings of engineering and clerical time, as well as its accuracy and consistency,
makes UnivEl a significant tool for management control. UnivEl thus
makes obsolete the traditional predetermined times data approaches
to work measurement.

UnivEl automatically generates time and method descriptions for
all manual operations that the normal operator will require to complete the task within the time allowed. The procedures have been
validated by many thousands of standards now in use in a wide
variety of industries. The controversial aspects of performance leveling, or rating, have been eliminated.

UnivEl has other advantages over a predetermined time system
in that it is not necessary to analyze each micromotion and write
the method description. That is done by the use of a simple coding
sheet. The information is then reduced to punched cards and fed
into the computer. The computer is programmed to print out the
complete method description, including time for each element and
frequency of occurrence of both repetitive and noncyclic elements,
add necessary allowances, and summarize the information into a standard expressed in decimal hours, decimal minutes, and pieces per
hour. All this is done at computer speed.

UnivEl is also compatible with the use of machining and process
formulas. Any algebraic formula that can be developed to cover machining, fabricating, welding, assembly, or any other process can be

---

[1] UnivEl and UniForm are registered trademarks. The following information
concerning UnivEl and UniForm has been furnished through the courtesy of
Parker Dumbauld, PE, Vice-President of Management Science, Inc., Appleton,
Wisconsin, and is printed with permission.

programmed into the computer. All that is required to use the formula is that the analyst specify the formula number and enter the controlling variables. The computer then makes the proper calculations and includes the elemental description and the proper time allowances in the printout just as it does a regular UnivEl element.

Thus, the system gives a detailed method instruction in the printout, and the method is pinned down to substantiate any methods changes that may occur at a later date. The computer is also programmed for the proper handling of simultaneous elements. The element taking the longer time is called the limiting element, and the element marked SIM, which takes less time to perform, is called the limited element. The computer is also programmed to indicate, but not include in the totals, internal manual operations to be done during process time.

Another advantage of the UnivEl system is that by using the computer it is possible to easily and quickly determine the best of several alternatives. As many different methods can be entered as are under consideration for the same operation, and the computer will determine which method takes the least amount of time. The technique provides valuable assistance to the methods or manufacturing engineer. In particular, it is well adapted to computerized assembly line balancing.

It must be emphasized that UnivEl and the computer will not perform methods analysis. The analyst must select the best method, keep distances to a minimum, and adhere to all the rules of work simplification. Time is always determined by method.

Appendix B illustrates the development of a standard time for a punch press operation by UnivEl.

UniForm. Whereas UnivEl is used mostly for repetitive operations, UniForm is generally used for nonrepetitive operations. However, they complement each other in that each can provide a valuable basis for input to and application of the other system. UniForm can be defined as an advanced statistical regression analysis developed for computer use.

Through the use of UniForm, the analyst determines all the causes or variables that may be responsible for, or describe in some measure, the end result. Since the effect of the various causes is not initially predictable, all possible causes that can be quantified, together with the quantified result, are entered into the UniForm analysis. The computer then determines the importance of the causes in the prediction of the effect.

Some of the causes may not at first sight appear to be related to the effect; therefore, any possible cause should be introduced to the computer and the computer will determine the relationship. Often there exists a functional relationship that is too complicated to grasp or describe in simple terms. There may be no sensible physical relationship between the variables, but it may be desirable to relate the variables by some sort of mathematical equation. The mathematical and statistical methods used in UniForm are not new; only the massive mathematical and computational requirements for formula development have deterred the use of the technique. The development and use of high-speed computers has led to the elimination of tedious and time-consuming computations and has placed a long-sought and practical technique in the hands of the industrial engineer.

All conventional time measurement techniques are based on the premise that a job is repetitive and that unit time values of the work elements will account for measured output. UniForm accepts the fact that certain jobs consist of nonrepetitive activities and that total performance can be more completely described by means of a weighted mathematical model or formula that contains the explanatory variables that describe the work. The result is a mathematical formula or model with which to measure the operation.

UniForm is also used to develop mathematical models of products to determine total cost, price, labor cost, and material cost. It can be used to analyze existing systems of costing and pricing to determine where and to what magnitude inaccuracies occur. It is an excellent tool for measuring, estimating, or analyzing any multivariant problem. It is fast and is not limited to work measurement alone. Examples of a few areas in which the method has been effectively applied are:

- Setting daywork or incentive standards for indirect operations
- Predetermining machine efficiency by using machine setting as variables
- Evaluating operator performance on assembly lines
- Determining the causes of high overhead costs
- Forecasting sales demand
- Determining of manpower utilization
- Determining crew size requirements
- Estimating costs
- Determining the resultant of a multivariant mix of quantifiable causes

Appendix C illustrates the development of a multivariant formula for an order-filling department by the use of UniForm. This is a significant example of a fairly common type of operation in which the determination of standards by conventional time study and standard data development would be not only initially very expensive but costly to administer. Those systems would require daily recording of details of work done in numerous categories and complicated timekeeping and would provide little possibility of auditing what work elements had actually been accomplished.

The UniForm techniques used are low in initial development cost, and the administrative cost is negligible because the sample formula uses data that are currently available and readily verified. In addition, the accuracy of the formula is well within acceptable limits for work measurement standards.

Standards Department Status

The new techniques discussed here have significantly altered the status of standards work; formerly considered to be a clerical function, it has now developed as a recognized profession. The proper recognition of this new status by management is closely related to the success of the wage incentive plan. We cannot get around the fact that, in assigning the wage incentive and work measurement responsibility to him, management has given the industrial engineer or his counterpart the responsibility for directing the expenditure of a very large portion of its payroll dollar and seeing to it that the firm receives maximum attainable productivity from its expenditure.

When the standards staff receives merited recognition by management and is considered an integral part of upper management echelons, the usual result is a smoothly operating incentive plan. On the other hand, if the work measurement function is considered as a minor clerical duty and the rate setter is relegated to obscure posts in the factory and seldom consulted on any matters of wage incentive policy, if his time studies are frequently disregarded, and if his rates are overruled by management in attempting to settle grievances related to incentives, then it is a safe prediction that the entire incentive plan is headed for serious trouble.

With the new tools available, the properly qualified industrial engineer is in a position to perform highly important technical and staff functions for use in management planning and decision making, particularly in the areas related to manufacturing. These techniques, while closely related to work measurement and wage incentives, have significant values for other management decisions and controls also.

Labor cost control, for example, must rely on accurate times for all activities. Those times are also the foundation for any preplanning and scheduling of production. The accuracy of such plans and schedules is completely dependent on the accuracy of the input data, that is, standard times. Writers of management articles who stress the need for management planning and control are inconsistent when they understate the necessity for accurate time standards for the activities that they would control.

It is significant that there is a strong correlation between a high level of industrial engineering performance and a high level of performance in the general manufacturing function. The question of to whom the chief industrial engineer should report is of general interest; he should be responsible to the highest manufacturing level. What is more important than that is the respect and status accorded to industrial engineering by the entire management group. As a general rule, management seems to get about the degree of industrial engineering competence that it attempts to attract with money and with recognition of industrial engineering as a vital part of the manufacturing function.

Appendix A

A Sample
Wage Incentive Policy

THE BASIC PURPOSE of any wage incentive plan is threefold: First, to develop ways and means of manufacturing a product at the least possible cost by careful analysis, study and measurement of manufacturing methods with due consideration for proper quality and proper labor relations. Second, to provide employees with an opportunity to increase their earnings through increased effort, application of skill, and proficiency. Third, to design the whole program as a control for manufacturing and labor costs, such controls thus becoming a part of or a byproduct of the program. Any plan that does not accomplish these results, either by reason of improper design or improper administration, will ultimately fail, usually with serious impairment of the company's competitive position, its labor relations, or both.

Therefore, it is the policy of the ABC Company to use incentives wherever the above conditions can be reasonably met. This means that incentives will be applied under the following conditions:

1. The work must be standardized and reasonably measurable by conventional industrial engineering techniques.

2. There must be assurance that acceptable standards of quality can be maintained.

3. There must be assurance that a sound incentive rate can be established which will be fair both to the company and the employees.

4. There must be assurance that reporting of completed work is

subject to verification by normal timekeeping procedures or other factory records.

5. There must be assurance that the operator will not be penalized, or conversely, derive excessive earnings, due to conditions beyond his control.

6. The cost of administering the plan will not outweight the benefits to be derived.

The basic contributing factor to increased productive output is the use of proper methods. This factor is far more significant as it affects rates of production than variations in the operator's effort and application. It is the basic controlling factor involved in the determination of incentive wages and is also the most difficult to standardize and control. Responsibility for initial development of proper methods is a function of the department supervisor, with staff assistance from Industrial Engineering. The maintenance and consistent application of methods so developed is the full responsibility of the supervisor. It is also the supervisor's responsibility to promptly report changes in methods within his department to Industrial Engineering, so that any necessary adjustments, either up or down, can be made to the incentive rates affected. Neglect of this simple factor has been the major reason for most failures of incentive plans, regardless of how technically sound they may have been when initially developed. It must also be recognized that in order to discharge this responsibility, the supervisor must have ready access to data outlining the exact methods used in support of the incentive rates for each operation in his department.

Today's manufacturing processes are subject to continuous change and improvement; some of these are major and easily recognized, many others are of a minor nature but, on the aggregate, frequently result in major changes in rates of production over a period of time. Those changes which tend to reduce production are usually reported promptly, while minor changes, or an accumulation of them, which tend to improve production, are often taken for granted and are not brought to the attention of Industrial Engineering. As a result, the general tendency of the incentive structure is to become looser with the passage of time. When this occurs, the company frequently ends up paying incentive wages for performance which in many cases is below daywork levels. Therefore, the proper administration of any wage incentive plan demands careful and planned auditing of all rates, on time schedules based on the frequency and importance of the specific operations, so that any changes in methods, tooling, materials, etc. can be promptly measured and the rates properly adjusted.

A further requirement of incentive maintenance is adequate control and auditing of the timekeeping function. The advantages of a wage incentive plan can easily be nullified by abuses such as miscounts, added allowances at day rate for functions that may be included in the rates, such as material handling, inspection, poor operator performance, or the payment of average earnings for certain nonincentive work.

Consistent with the above policy, the following general procedures will be applied by the Industrial Engineering Department:

1. Incentive rates will be applied on an individual basis wherever possible. Group incentives will generally be used only in situations where output is dependent on close cooperation between employees, or when it is difficult to segregate individual performance and counts.

2. Rates may be established through the use of time study, standard data, predetermined times, work sampling, or other accepted Industrial Engineering techniques.

3. Established incentive rates will not be altered except for changes in methods, tooling, materials, job conditions, or for correction of clerical or computational errors. Such changes, when they occur, will be explained to the employees involved.

4. Incentive rates will be audited periodically to insure their compatibility with conditions actually in use at the time. Any adjustments indicated by these audits, either up or down, will be made in accordance with paragraph 2 above.

5. Incentive gains must be earned, never guaranteed.

6. Incentive earnings will be limited only by the employee's ability and willingness to perform acceptable work in excess of standard requirements.

7. The computation of incentive rates will be based on an earnings opportunity of 30 percent for the average experienced operator, with normal skills, using prescribed methods and when working at incentive pace. However, failure to achieve such earnings does not by itself, indicate that the rate is inadequate.

8. Temporary rates may be issued at the discretion of the Industrial Engineering Department to apply to work which has not been standardized, or where the length of the run does not justify normal work measurement procedures. Such rates will show a cancellation date, usually 30 days after date of issue, after which they cannot be applied without special approval from the Industrial Engineering Department. Such temporary rates are not to be used as a basis for comparison or consistency with established permanent rates.

Appendix B

Development of a UnivEl Standard[1]

THIS EXAMPLE of the development of a UnivEl standard, for forming an aluminum blank to profile, is intended to show in detail the development of a UnivEl rate for a punch press operation. Figure 23 illustrates the UnivEl coding sheet which the analyst uses to record the basic information describing the operation. Key punch cards are prepared from this sheet and then fed into the computer, which then prints out the complete operation description and the standard times. The upper portion of the coding sheet has the usual information on customer code, part description, material descriptions, machine number, operation number as well as a complete description of the operation, in this case "Form to Profile Right and Left."

Columns 1, 2, 3 and 4. Numerals placed here are used to identify the element descriptions by the corresponding line numbers on the computer printout.

Columns 5 to 15. In columns 5 to 15 the analyst enters manual element types, their level (characteristics), conditions, and locations by use of a simple numerical code. For example, consider the example of moving a box from a table to a location on the floor. The person doing this job must first obtain control of the box itself. He must

---

[1] Thanks are due Management Science, Inc., Appleton, Wisconsin, for supplying this material and permitting its use here.

174

Figure 23. A UnivEl coding sheet.

UnivEl® CODING SHEET

CUST CODE: YOUR COMPANY, ANYWHERE, U.S.A.

ENGR: J. N. G.

MO DA YR: 41 817Ø

PART DESCRIPTION: PRESS FORMED PANEL — 1

MATERIAL DESCRIPTION: 16 GAUGE ALUMINUM BLANKS

DEPT NO. 24 | MACH NO. 1110S | OPER NO. 20

OPERATION DESCRIPTION: FORM TO PROFILE - RIGHT & LEFT — 3

TOOLING-PART USED: 24 1110S | 20 17146 DIE AND 112146 BLANKS — 7

PART NUMBER: 1246-1AX | WT-LBS 1/14 | BRN — 9

REMARKS: SEE NOTES ON PRINT

PART NUMBER: IN — NUMBER — X USED | ALL CARDS — 5

CUST CODE	ELEMENT TYPE	JU V E L 0/A	CONDITIONS LOCATIONS	DISTANCES FT. IN. DEC.	EFF.-NET WEIGHT	CONT. DIM.	DEGREES OR TURNS	FREQUENCY	*	VARIABLES — LITERALS	COM	COM FREQ.	DECIMAL HOURS	DECIMAL MINUTES
		/ / /	4 / 18	.14					, BLANKS, SEPARATORS				U
2		/ / /	5 / 3Ø	.14 / 16					, FIRST BLANK, POSITION IN DIE				U
3		/ / /	5 / 2	.14 / 16					, SECOND BLANK, POSITION IN DIE				U
4		/ / /	2 / 3Ø	.12					, BOTH HANDS, PRESS BUTTONS				U
5	COM; PRESS; TIME AT 3Ø STROKES PER MINUTE													U
6		/ / /	2 3 / 3Ø	.14 / 16					· PIECES, DIE, EACH PIECE, STACK				U
7	COM; THE FOLLOWING ELEMENTS DESCRIBE THE STOCK UP OF BLA													U
8	COM - NKS & MOVEMENT OF FINISHED PARTS TO CHUTES													U
9		/ 2 / 2	3 2 / 2 4	.918 / 6					, 14, STACK, LEFT, SIDE, STACK, CHUTE				U
1Ø		/ 2 2 2	3 2 / 7 2	.918 / 6					, 14, STACK, RIGHT, SIDE, STACK, CHUTE				U
11		/ 2 2 2	5 2 / 6 Ø	.918 / 6					, 14, BLANKS, STOCK, THEM, SEPARATORS				U
13	END													

	F I O R	*	FOR. NO.	A	B	C	D	E	F	G	H	J	K	L	M	N	O	P	Q
12	F I O R		9 Ø Ø 9																Ø 3 3
	F I O R																		
	F I O R																		U

*CODE: · COMPUTE, PRINT SUBTOTAL & CLEAR ; COMPUTE, PRINT TIME SEPARATE FROM
COMPUTE AND ACCUMULATE TIME , ACCUMULATION
? SIMO — COMPARE TO FOLLOWING ELEMENT ; COMPUTE CURRENT TOTAL
: COMPUTE & PRINT SUBTOTAL & CLEAR : COMPUTE & PRINT CURRENT TOTAL

COPYRIGHT © 1967 MANAGEMENT SCIENCE INC. APPLETON, WISCONSIN

UniAtion

then remove the box from the table and set it on the floor. If he is using traditional manual techniques, the analyst must consider many aspects of this job individually. What is the class of reach and move? How difficult is the grasp? What is the class of fit? Is a side step involved?

UnivEl makes such micromotion analysis obsolete by considering the job conditions that dictate the motion pattern. Combinations of movements are referred to as job levels and are expressed to the computer with a single-digit code number. The degree of movement such as a hand handle to the side and down is referred to as a job condition and is expressed by a single-digit code number. The system also allows for determination of simultaneous elements and other similar situations. The point is that the computer takes such job-coded information and generates the time needed for the motion patterns required. Since combinations of only 23 numerical codes are used, the system is extremely simple to learn and use.

Columns 16 to 27. Distances involved in the element are indicated in columns 16 to 27. The computer considers these distances in developing the standard time for the element, and the distances also appear on the printout sheet.

Columns 28 to 37. In columns 28 to 37 the analyst enters other variables: weight, the controlling dimension, and the number of degrees or turns where applicable. This information again is used by the computer in determining the elemental time.

Columns 38 to 41. Frequency, the number of times a specific element may occur in a complete operation, is indicated in columns 38 to 41. The computer multiplies the elemental time derived for such an individual element by the number of times it occurs and includes this time in the complete operation summary.

Column 42. An entry in column 42 instructs the computer how to utilize the information. For example, a comma tells the computer to compute and accumulate the time; a period tells the computer to compute, print, subtotal, and clear. Similar elements in the code appear in the lower right-hand portion of the coding sheet.

Columns 43 to 79. The remaining columns are largely concerned with literals, that is, the addition of specific nominal terms. For example, if blanks were not specified, the computer would merely print "object." The literals appearing on this coding sheet can be easily recognized on the printout. At the bottom of the sheet, line 12 refers to formula 9009, which in this application tells the computer to add 4.5 percent allowances to the standard previously developed.

The coding sheet thus described is all that is required to be filled

Figure 24. A UnivEl methods instruction sheet.

YOUR COMPANY, ANYWHERE, U.S.A.   PART NO. 1246-AX

PART DESCRIPTION PRESS FORMED PANEL   OPERATION NO. 20
MATERIAL DESCRIPTION 16 GAUGE ALUMINUM BLANKS   MACH. NO. 1105 DEPT. NO. 24   WT. 1.4 LBS.   BRW

TOOLING OR PART USED 1746 DIE AND 1246 BLANKS   USED X   OPER. DESC. FORM TO PROFILE - RIGHT & LEFT

REMARKS SEE NOTES ON PRINT   ENGR. J.N.G.   DATE 4/08/70

NO.	ELEMENT DESCRIPTION	FREQ.	HRS/PC	MIN/PC
001	OBT. BLANKS FROM SEPARATORS 8 IN DIST.	1.00	.000190	.0114
002	MOVE FIRST BLANK TO POSITION IN DIE 30 IN DIST.	1.00	.000608	.0365
003	MOVE SECOND BLANK TO POSITION IN DIE 2 IN DIST.	1.00	.000302	.0181
004	MOVE BOTH HANDS TO PRESS BUTTONS 30 IN DIST.	1.00	.000365	.0219
005	PRESS TIME AT 30 STROKES PER MINUTE	1.00	.000550	.0330
006	OBT. PIECES FROM DIE 30 IN DIST, MOVE EACH PIECE TO STACK 12 IN DIST.	1.00	.000526	.0316
		SUB-T	.002541	.1525
	THE FOLLOWING ELEMENTS DESCRIBE THE STOCK UP OF BLANKS & MOVEMENT OF FINISHED PARTS TO CHUTES			
007	OBT. STACK FROM LEFT SIDE 24 IN DIST, MOVE STACK TO SIDE TO CHUTE 64 IN DIST.	0.14	.000135	.0081
008	OBT. STACK AT SIDE FROM RIGHT SIDE 72 IN DIST, MOVE STACK TO SIDE TO CHUTE 72 IN DIST.	0.14	.000218	.0131
009	OBT. BLANKS AT SIDE FROM STOCK 60 IN DIST, MOVE THEM TO SIDE TO SEPARATORS 22 IN DIST.	0.14	.000146	.0088
		TOTAL	.003040	.1825
			.000136	.0082

9009   4.5 PER CENT ALLOW.   TOTAL .003176 .1907

.003176 HRS/PC   314.9 PCS/HOUR

PG.01

out by the analyst. When the information has been key-punched and the punch cards have been fed into the computer, the computer produces the methods instruction sheet shown in Figure 24. Note that this printout shows the hours per piece and the minutes per piece for each element as well as noncyclic elements, computes the total time with allowances, and prints the standard in terms of hours per piece and pieces per hour. These printouts can be made available to the shop. They then present a valuable device for comparing existing methods with those contemplated in the development of the standard.

The example presented in this appendix shows the basic UnivEl time generator and translator with a simple allowance formula. UnivEl also includes many other options that supplement the one described and provide the industrial engineer with tools to generate time standards for any combination of man-machine activities.

Appendix C

Development of a
Formula by Use of UniForm[1]

THE SOLUTION to a multivariant activity described in this appendix has many applications for so-called unmeasurable jobs such as shipping, receiving, warehousing, tool control, material handling, maintenance, and much office work. In this particular instance, which involved order filling and packing for a large wholesale distributor, it was determined that the variables were number of orders, total number of pounds, total number of pieces, and total number of packages. Fifteen samplings were taken, together with the actual number of man-minutes required, as shown in Table 9.

An analysis of the input data by the usual graphical methods indicated that there was no discernible relationship between any of the four variables and the actual time required; see Figures 25 to 28. However, when these input data were fed into the computer programmed for the UniForm procedure, the following formula, expressed in man-minutes, was developed:

Packing time = 12.17 + .1487 × (No. of orders) + .0084 × (No. of pounds)
+ .0187 × (No. of pieces) + .1030 × (No. of packages)

The multiple coefficient of this formula is 0.931, and the standard

[1] Copyrighted by Management Science, Inc., Appleton, Wisconsin. Reproduced by permission.

179

Table 9. Input data for order-filling formula.

Sample	Orders	Pounds	Pieces	Packages	Man-Minutes
1	7	45	120	6	441
2	2	70	40	28	465
3	16	10	90	4	473
4	10	100	55	12	474
5	4	130	20	20	416
6	12	50	48	11	450
7	8	90	69	9	437
8	15	26	52	10	447
9	4	115	35	22	466
10	9	20	60	14	423
11	3	55	58	24	459
12	14	80	50	5	425
13	6	25	105	12	435
14	8	35	70	17	464
15	11	105	82	4	458

Figure 25. Plot of total orders against time.

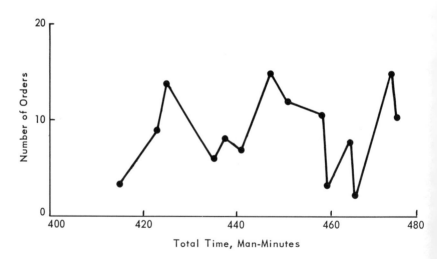

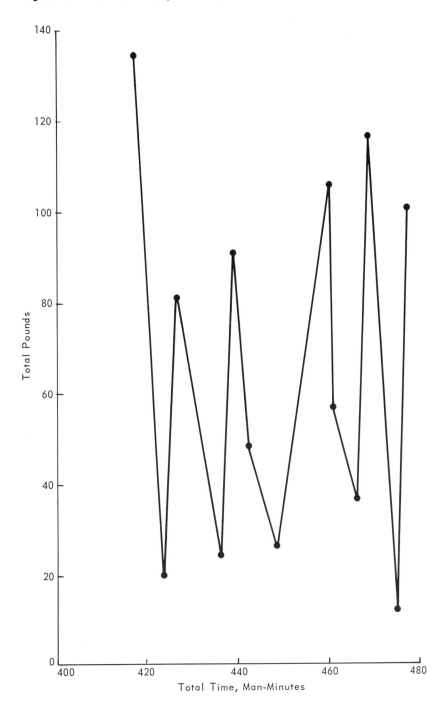

Figure 26. Plot of total pounds against time.

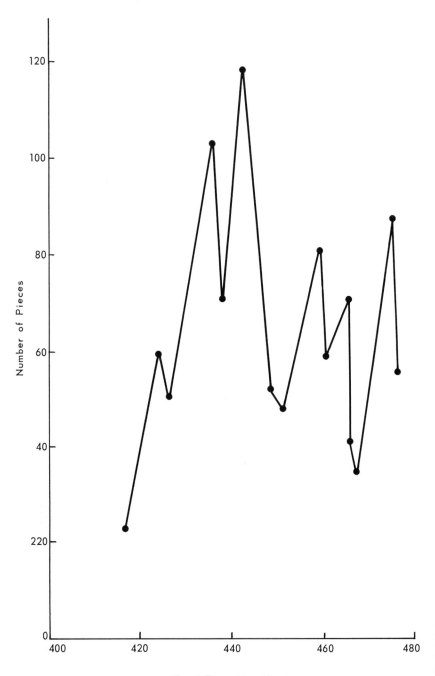

Figure 27. Plot of total pieces against time.

Figure 28. Plot of total packages against time.

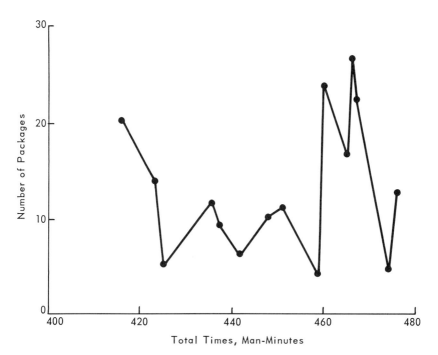

Total Times, Man-Minutes

Table 10. Comparison of calculated times and actual times for order-filling formula.

Sample	Actual Times	Calculated Times	Residual
1	441	440.84	0.16
2	465	464.17	0.83
3	473	468.35	4.65
4	474	471.78	2.22
5	416	424.64	−8.64
6	450	435.96	14.04
7	437	428.96	8.64
8	447	457.54	−10.54
9	466	460.70	5.30
10	423	419.44	3.56
11	459	458.94	0.06
12	425	432.96	−7.96
13	435	442.78	−7.78
14	464	466.84	−2.84
15	458	459.09	−1.09

Figure 29. Times calculated by UniForm formula compared with actual times.

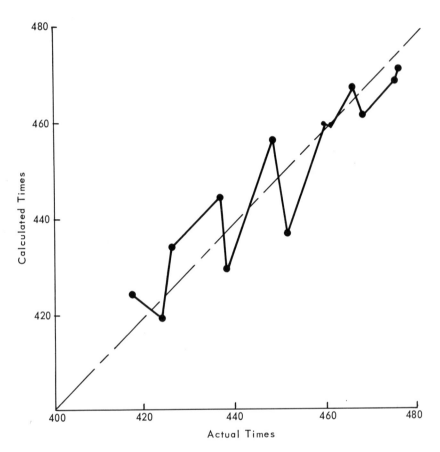

error of estimate is 8.056. Figure 29 represents graphically the close correlation between estimated times as developed by the formula and the actual times developed by the 15 inputs. Table 10 shows the same information in tabular form with the actual times compared to estimated times as developed by the formula. The maximum difference between actual and calculated times (actual, 450; calculated, 435.96) is slightly over 3 percent, which is well within accepted limits of accuracy for most conventional standards development.

Appendix D

Uses of Work Measurement

WORK MEASUREMENT has a multiplicity of applications; it is a necessity even in the absence of a wage incentive system. Sound standards are vital to any program concerned with the functioning and management of an industrial enterprise. There is a continuing need to improve standards so they can be used with confidence in broad management decisions.

However, the potential value of standards decreases rapidly as the standards become inaccurate by reason of failure to adjust them for continuing improvements in shop methods and technology. That is particularly true in this time of computer application to such management areas as production control, scheduling, and costing. The value of computer applications is dependent on the accuracy and validity of the input data, that is, the standards. If they are unreliable or inaccurate, the value of the computer is nullified. This important relationship between standards and the computer has developed the popular expression "garbage in—garbage out."

Typical Standards Utilizations

1. Production planning
   Machine loading
   Capacity analysis

Routing
Machine availability
2. Work force planning
Hiring, training, transfers, layoffs
Balancing work force with existing schedules
3. Production scheduling
Delivery promises
Scheduling of material purchases and deliveries
Scheduling work through the plant
Scheduling tooling
Estimating time factors for future work
4. Production control
Progress reporting and control (actual completion versus planned completion)
5. Inventory control
Evaluating work in process inventory
Determining factory float
6. Facilities planning
Planning economic machine utilization (number of shifts, days per week, high fixed cost mechanization versus high variable labor costs)
Establishing plant and machine capacity
Establishing equipment requirements
Establishing tool, jig, and fixture requirements
Evaluating improvements
Evaluating replacements
Scheduling the building or acquisition of new plants or facilities
Development and evaluation of automation projects
Comparing alternate manufacturing methods
7. Plant layout
Determining space requirements (work and storage)
Determining number of machines needed in a work center
Establishing size and location of storage areas
8. Work methods
Improving operator performance
Eliminating conditions that cause fatigue
9. Operating management problems
Balancing production and assembly lines
Assigning work
Equipping lines (jigs, fixtures, tools)
Evaluating operator performance

      Assigning workers for best performance
      Evaluating non-incentive work
      Measuring indirect work and manpower utilization

10. Marketing and selling
      Quoting prices to customers
      Evaluating cost-price-volume interplay

11. Cost accounting
      Establishing standard product costs
      Implementing cost control and cost reduction
      Evaluating and allocating indirect expense
      Make versus buy decision making
      Estimating costs of new products
      Evaluating alternate designs for new products

12. Industrial relations
      Resolving rate grievances and union claims
      Determining facts relating to union disputes

13. Motivation
      Wage incentives—direct and indirect workers
      Establishing measured daywork standards
      Establishing supervisory incentives
      Performance standards as factors in merit rating

Index